More About Mark

John Fenton was born in Liverpool in 1921, the son of an Anglican clergyman. He was educated at St Edward's School, Queen's College, Oxford, and Lincoln Theological College. After ordination in 1944, he served as a curate in Wigan and then as a member of the staff of Lincoln Theological College (1947–54), before his appointment as vicar of Wentworth, South Yorkshire (1954–8). He was principal of Lichfield Theological College, then of St Chad's College, Durham, before becoming a canon of Christ Church, Oxford, in 1978. He retired in 1992 and lives in Oxford; he is the author of a number of books on the New Testament.

Marco filio meo
medico carissimo

More About Mark

John Fenton

Published in Great Britain in 2001 by
Society for Promoting Christian Knowledge
Holy Trinity Church
Marylebone Road
London NW1 4DU

British Library Cataloguing-in-Publication Data

A catalogue record for this book is available from the British Library

ISBN 0-281-05452-5

Typeset by Kenneth Burnley, Wirral, Cheshire
Printed in Great Britain by
Antony Rowe Ltd, Chippenham, Wiltshire

Contents

Preface

Seven of the pieces gathered together here have previously appeared in print. They have all been revised to some extent.

My thanks are due to the following, who have kindly allowed me to collect these papers for republication:

Brother Tristam, editor of the *Franciscan*.
Dr Richard Burridge, Dean of King's College, London.
The Reverend David Cruise, of the West London Mission.
Dr William Jacob, editor of *Theology*.
Canon James Butterworth, editor of *The Reality of God*.
Dr Stephen Barton, editor of *Resurrection*.
Dr Ernest Nicholson, the Provost of Oriel College, Oxford.
Canon Hugh Wybrew, the Vicar of St Mary Magdalen,
    Oxford.

I must also thank Professor Leslie Houlden for continuous advice and encouragement, Ruth McCurry, Mary Matthews and David Sanders at SPCK for their patience and help, and my wife for much typing.

JOHN FENTON
Oxford

1

Introduction:
My Life with Mark

I T ALL BEGAN WITH Robert Henry Lightfoot, but I never really understood why. I was in my second year at Queen's College, Oxford, reading theology, and my college tutor, E. C. Ratcliff, decided to send me to Lightfoot for New Testament tutorials. Ratcliff was a man of extensive knowledge and, like many other theology tutors at that time, could perfectly well cope with the whole of the syllabus, from Genesis to the Council of Chalcedon. So it was that in my second and third years I would make the journey along Queen's Lane to what was then the main entrance to New College, with the ink of my weekly essay drying as I went.

Lightfoot had been the Bampton Lecturer in 1934 (*History and Interpretation in the Gospels*, 1935) and he had published *Locality and Doctrine in the Gospels* in 1938. He was an outstanding teacher and his tutorials were occasions you would never forget. You and he sat side by side at a table and he read your essay himself, making tiny pencil-marks in the left-hand margin of your page. When he had thus gone through the whole of your essay silently, he would say something like: 'Thank you very much for this. I found it extremely interesting. May I, though, possibly make one or two comments?' And he would then go back to the passages he had marked and discuss all the problems that were raised there, and the others that were not but should have been. He would also bring to your notice any mistakes or infelicities or ambiguities in your English grammar and syntax. Towards the end of the hour, he would ask: 'What will you write about next week?' and it was up to you to choose for yourself. I remember, on

1

one occasion, 'Some *gar* clauses in Mark', and on another 'Fear and amazement in Mark'. We did not bother about a syllabus; the examination schools were a long way ahead, or so it seemed at the time, and we were far more interested in the subject than in any future examination papers. In order to get as much as possible out of Lightfoot, I chose New Testament textual criticism for my special subject in the final school.

At this time, Lightfoot was regarded by the majority of those who were writing on the New Testament and teaching it, in England, as a man who held unusual views. For example, he maintained that Mark had intentionally ended his book with the words:

They said nothing to anyone, for they were afraid. (Mark 16.8)

Lightfoot believed, almost alone of those who were writing on this subject in England at that time, that there never had been an ending of the Gospel that had been lost; Nero's police had not arrested the evangelist at the moment he completed this famous line; nor was it the case that Mark had always intended to say more, but could never get round to doing so.

The standard books on the Synoptic Gospels that were available at that time were Streeter's *Four Gospels* (1924), Rawlinson's commentary on Mark in *The Westminster Commentaries* (1925) and the writings of F. C. Burkitt, V. Taylor, T. W. Manson and C. H. Dodd. I had not found much inspiration coming at me from them. Mark was, to them, a person who had written down what he could remember of Peter's reminiscences, as Papias had said. The Greek in which Mark wrote his Gospel lacked style, and he was (fortunately, one was expected to believe) free from any contamination through having ideas of his own, or of anyone else; a clean pipe, through which tradition could flow without being contaminated. This was part of what was then known as the Marcan Hypothesis, and it still held sway in Oxford and in the rest of England, apart from the books and lectures and tutorials of Lightfoot. There was, however, a single ray of light coming from the west: a small book by J. H. Ropes of Harvard, *The Synoptic Gospels* (1934), which Lightfoot admired and to which he referred in the published text of the Bampton Lectures in 1935 (p. 109 n. 1).

The other major influence on me, at that time (1940–3) was Søren Kierkegaard, whose writings were being published here. I bought them all, and W. Lowrie's *Life*, as they came out in English translation from the Oxford University Press.

During my year as a student at Lincoln Theological College (1943–4) I was introduced by the Warden, E. S. Abbott, to writers such as the English fourteenth-century mystics, Richard Rolle, the author of *The Cloud of Unknowing*, Walter Hilton and Julian of Norwich; and to the Spanish mystics, Teresa of Avila and John of the Cross. I thought I could see a connection of some sort between them and their master, Pseudo-Dionysius, on the one hand, and Mark on the other. In all of them, it seemed, there was a stress on faith as darkness, and a distrust of miracles.

One of the events at Lincoln was a course of lectures delivered during the week before Holy Week; Holy Week was a retreat, and the lectures in the previous week (the Passiontide Lectures) were intended to provide us with something to think about during the coming time of silence. In 1944, the lecturer was Austin Farrer, at that time Fellow and Chaplain of Trinity College, Oxford, and his subject was 'The Passion Narrative in Mark'. Among many fascinating points, he suggested that the words of the centurion in Mark 15.39 could be read as the final dismissal of the whole event of the crucifixion: 'He really was the Son of God – I don't think.' Mark had kept up the irony to the end of the book.

Austin Farrer's Bampton Lectures for 1948, 'The Glass of Vision', included a discussion of the ending of Mark's Gospel, which was, in general, not well received; nor was his later book, *A Study in St Mark* (1951); the tide had not yet turned, and the Marcan Hypothesis had not yet been demolished. R. Bultmann's *Theology of the New Testament* (1948–53; ET 1952–5) had no place for the synoptic evangelists as theologians. Vincent Taylor's commentary on Mark (1953) also had little time for Mark as a theologian. 'What we find in Mark is no superimposed dogmatic construction, but the virile ideas of Jesus Himself' (p. 125). On the other hand, Farrer continued to explain what sort of a book he thought Mark was, and what Matthew had done to Mark, in *St Matthew and St Mark* (1954, second edition 1966). Lightfoot himself had returned to the question of the ending of the Gospel and to other questions of interpretation in *The Gospel Message of St Mark* (1950). He died in 1953, and a volume of essays was published in his memory (*Studies in the Gospels*, edited by D. E. Nineham) in 1955. This was probably the moment when the tide began to turn, and Lightfoot began to be regarded as the author of books that were read and quoted more widely and with greater appreciation. The first book I wrote was on the Marcan passion and resurrection (*Preaching the Cross*, 1958), for those who were to preach on Good Friday and Easter Day. On the Continent, Bornkamm and Conzelmann were thought to have invented redaction criticism, but to us in England what they were saying was largely Lightfoot's ideas and methods, without acknowledgement.

Why did Mark's Gospel and Lightfoot's interpretation of it appeal to me so much? Was there anything that predisposed me to find this short and strange book so fascinating?

One answer that I can hear to these questions goes as follows: 'You were brought up in a heavily clerical family. Your grandfather and his brother-in-law, your father and his three brothers, one brother of your mother and two of your first cousins, were all Anglican clergymen. You yourself never considered any other profession seriously. You are, as far as can be seen now, the last in your family to be ordained. But from the first you were determined to be different from all the others. That is why you became such an enthusiastic reader of Søren Kierkegaard during your undergraduate days in Oxford, with emphasis on offence, irony, Christ the stumbling-block and the foolishness of God. This is why Lightfoot became your hero, with his unusual and revolutionary views on Mark. This is why you found John of the Cross attractive: he was so negative; he was Luther in Catholic disguise.

'In the 1930s and 1940s many people turned to communism in order to define themselves as different from the majority; you turned to unpopular forms of New Testament scholarship and to the spirituality of the Via Negativa. You interpreted Mark as an outsider who portrayed the Twelve as failures and Jesus as the one who made no impression upon anyone; whose resurrection was not reported to any of the disciples by the women because they remained silent. You found salvation in a certain way of reading Mark, while others were finding it in Marx.

'Your attitude to Mark began as a late-adolescent fixation; the trouble with you is that you have never grown up.'

All of this is probably true, and there is no point in denying it. The only thing that can be said about it is that it is irrelevant. One of the major themes of Mark's book is that God makes use of human failures: the male disciples and the female disciples, the religious leaders and the Romans, the centurion who finally dismisses Jesus himself as a false pretender. We have the treasure in earthen vessels, and it does not matter that they are earthen. God's power is made known in weakness. Mark was right to call his book Good News; it is Good News about God. Three times he says it:

Everything is possible to one who believes. (9.23)
Everything is possible for God. (10.27)
Abba, Father, everything is possible to you. (14.36)

Mark's Gospel invites the reader into a new world, where we are no longer merely the victims of our upbringing and the accidents of our personalities, because there is a God who is omnipotent; and he reveals his omnipotence in the story Mark tells of human ignorance, misunderstanding, fear and weakness. In this paradox lies the secret of the fascination and applicability of Mark's book.

The papers collected together in this volume illustrate this theme, and show how one Gospel has been interpreted by one writer over the last thirty years.

'Why Are There Four Gospels?' was a paper read to the

Oxford Society of Historical Theology in October 1985. 'Preaching the Message of Jesus Now' appeared first in *The Franciscan* 14/4 (September 1972). 'John of the Cross and the Gospel According to Mark' is an abbreviated version of the seventh Eric Symes Abbott Memorial Lecture (May 1992). 'Mark's Gospel: The Oldest and the Best?' was delivered in a series of Hugh Price Hughes lectures on 'Explorations of Faith for the Twenty-First Century' in March 1999 and was published in *Theology* in March 2001. 'The Passion Narrative in Mark's Gospel' is from *The Reality of God: Essays in Honour of Tom Baker* (Severn House Publishers, 1986). 'The Ending of Mark's Gospel' is from *Resurrection: Essays in Honour of Leslie Houlden* (SPCK, 1994). 'Some Problems with Matthew' is a revised version of a paper read to a society in Oxford in 1999. 'The Blessed Virgin Mary' was a university sermon preached in Oriel College Chapel in March 1995. 'Eating People' is a revision of a paper read to a society in Oxford in February 1991 and was published in *Theology* in November of that year. 'Christ the King' was a sermon preached at the Church of St Mary Magdalen, Oxford, in November 1994.

2

Why Are There Four Gospels?

THEOLOGIANS, WE ARE ALWAYS BEING TOLD, should address themselves to the questions people ask and not to those in which no one is interested; and certainly there are enough questions being asked at the present time to keep us in full employment for several years. I cannot pretend that the problem I want to discuss is one that worries anybody. I cannot cross my heart and say that anyone I know has said to me, in the last month or so, 'What gets me down about Christianity is that you have four Gospels. If you had only one I could believe it.' In fact, come to think of it, I do not know that anybody has said that to me, ever. So, if the problem is not pressing, why bother with it?

First, because we shall understand the Gospels better if we can see them as individual instances in a series; the process that produced more than one Gospel will help us to understand what any one Gospel is. If we ignore the relationship in which they stand to one another, we shall miss much of what they are about.

Second, because we shall understand the Christian movement in the first and second centuries better if we pursue the question of the multiplicity of Gospels. The inability of second-century Christians to settle for one book will show us something about the way they thought, and how the movement operated.

And third, the answer we give to the question, Why are there four Gospels? will be different from the answer they themselves gave to the question, in the second century. Our answer will be different, and we cannot but think that it will be better; that is, nearer to the truth. If we were rash, we might say that we are the first people to know what the answer is to the question Why are there four Gospels? That alone makes the question interesting and, possibly, important.

But why is it that no one worries about there being four Gospels? It is odd that there are four; and it is even more odd that we have not been worried by it. Here are four books of narrative, that deal with the same main characters, set in the same period of time; but they do not agree on content or on order. Why does this not worry us?

We should find it hard to explain if British Telecom issued four *Phone Books* giving different numbers for the same people. We should know that we had a problem on our hands if Railtrack published different timetables for trains to London; or if a college lodge sold four different histories of the college, with the events of its past in different orders. Why have we not felt the same about the four Gospels?

The pressures on the Church to have only one book must have been powerful. Paul could be read as having said to the Galatians that there is no other gospel; and that could have been used as an argument for expressing the uniqueness of the gospel in the singleness of one volume, one narrative, one story. The type of statement that you find in Ephesians: There is one body and one Spirit, as there is also one hope held out in God's call to you; one Lord, one faith, one baptism; one God and Father of all – this kind of language, you might have thought, would easily have led people to saying, There is one gospel and no other, as there is also one book that the Church accepts. And we know that Tatian did in fact pursue this aim, and that he produced the *Diatessaron*, using John as the outline, and inserting material from the other three Gospels into the Johannine framework.

The continuing existence of the four separate Gospels somehow resisted all moves and pressures towards unity, in the sense of having only one book. No one was able to do with the Gospels what was done with the see of Peter: the Church could be defined in terms of communion with Rome, but no one said: There is only one book that contains the gospel. (Or if they did, they were reckoned to be heretics.) The question is, Why are we not more aware of this than I imagine we are?

First of all, for a practical reason: the way in which Gospels are experienced in church. They are read in fragments at the Sunday eucharist, or in sections at the offices, and little attention is paid to the announcement at the beginning of the reading. We do not say to ourselves, Aha, it's Matthew today, or Oh dear, another bit from John! The differences between the Gospels are not part of the consciousness of the normal churchgoer. Most people who attend a Sunday service are in the position of the curate in Samuel Butler's *The Way of All Flesh* (1903) who could not recount the resurrection appearances in Luke, but harmonized in the Matthean angel rolling back the stone and sitting on it.

The only occasion on which the differences between the Gospels are made obvious is Holy Week, when, in the Book of Common Prayer (1662), the passion narratives are read on consecutive days; then, the attentive reader might notice that Jesus' last words are different on Sunday and Tuesday from what they are on Thursday and again on Friday. But apart from this, Gospels are not presented as contradictory books; even the birth-stories in Matthew and Luke can be phased into one another and made into a single continuous narrative, with the joins discreetly covered by the singing of carols and Christmas hymns.

Second, it has been suggested that the differences between the Gospels are just what you would expect; witnesses never agree on what they have seen. Four people describing the same event in the street will disagree on the colour of the clothes worn by the suspect, his age, and whether he wore glasses. According to this explanation of the Gospels, their differences from each other are evidence for their genuineness; had the evangelists all agreed, they would be witnesses who had been tampered with. The fact that they contradict one another proves that they are independent of each other, and therefore all the more reliable. We have not just what one person saw, but what four people saw.

This explanation is much loved by lawyers, policemen, magistrates' clerks, lay members of the General Synod, and other such like persons. But it will not do. Once it is seen that there has been copying of one evangelist by another, their independent status is destroyed. Those lists of which miracle-stories come in one Gospel, or in two, or three, or all four, do not show which miracles are better attested; the only one that is put in the list of all four is the feeding of the five thousand, but we do not have four independent accounts of this event; probably not more than two (Mark's and John's); possibly only one (Mark's, which may have been copied by the other three). What might be called the Crown Court explanation of the differences between the Gospels must be abandoned by those who hold any of the standard solutions to the synoptic problem.

A third way of easing the difficulty of the multiplicity of Gospels is the suggestion that the four books are mutually complementary. You need all four, to hear the one gospel. The writers supplemented one another. At this point it is usual to distinguish between the original meaning of 'gospel', that is 'message', and the secondary meaning, 'a book containing the message'. Conventions have been introduced for printing, using a capital G for one or other. The thing that is said, however, is that there are four Gospels, but only one gospel; four books, one message.

This is, I suppose, the oldest explanation of the multiplicity. One form of it is the statement by Clement of Alexandria, quoted by Eusebius: 'But, last of all, John perceiving that the external facts [*ta sōmatika*] had been made plain in the Gospels, being urged by his friends and inspired by the Spirit, composed a spiritual Gospel [*pneumatikon euangelion*] (*Church History*, 6.14.7). In this way, the differences between the Gospels of Matthew, Mark and Luke on the one hand, and the Gospel of John on the other, are accounted for: the former contain the somatic facts, while the latter has the pneumatic significance; both are necessary, and they fit together happily, just as soma and pneuma comprise one person.

Another version of this explanation is that which is provided by Irenaeus in his book *Against Heresies* (3.11.7, 8). Heretics, he says, use the Gospels and base their peculiar doctrines on them. But they are one-Gospel men: the Ebionites use only Matthew; Marcion, a mutilated version of Luke; the followers of Cerinthus use Mark; and the Valentinians, John. Irenaeus then proceeds in a much-quoted passage:

> It is not possible that the Gospels can be either more or fewer in number than they are. For since there are four zones of the world in which we live, and four principal winds, while the Church is scattered throughout the world and the pillar and ground of the Church is the gospel and the spirit of life; it is fitting that she should have four pillars, breathing out immortality on every side, and vivifying men afresh. From which fact, it is evident that the Word, the Artificer of all, He that sitteth upon the cherubim, and containeth all things, He who was manifested to men, has given us the gospel under four aspects, but bound together by one Spirit.

He then goes on to relate the four Gospels to the four faces of the cherubim and the four living creatures in the Apocalypse; the lion is John's Gospel, because the lion stands for power and John begins with the creation of the world; the calf is Luke, because that Gospel begins with the sacrifice in the temple: the man is Matthew, because of the human genealogy at the beginning of it; and the eagle is Mark, because it begins with the Spirit coming down on Jesus at his baptism. The conclusion is that the living creatures are quadriform, and the gospel is quadriform, as is also the course followed by the Lord. Moreover, there are four covenants of God made with Adam, Noah, Moses and Christ.

An explanation of this kind (ex post facto rationalization) does not satisfy us, because we know that however many Gospels there had been, Irenaeus could have provided an equally convincing reason of this sort to justify it.

If there had been only one Gospel, he could have said that
   there is only one God and one holy, catholic and apostolic
   Church.
If there had been two Gospels, he could have related them
   to the two natures of Christ, or the two ages of the
   world.
If three, the three persons of the Godhead, or faith, hope and
   charity.
If five, the five books of Moses and the Psalms, or the five
   senses, or the fingers of the hand.
If six, the working days of creation and so also of re-creation.
If seven, the gifts of the Spirit, the planets, or the seven
   churches of the Apocalypse.
If eight, the number of perfection, being seven plus one.
If nine, the fruit of the Spirit from Galatians chapter 5.
If ten, the commandments given to Moses, or the fingers of
   two hands.
If eleven, those of the Twelve who went to heaven.
If twelve, the tribes of Israel, the apostles, or the months of
   the year.

If we were to be persuaded that Irenaeus's fours explain the
fact of there being four Gospels, we should have to know
something more than what he tells us: we should have to
know that at some point in time somebody was moved by the
number four to do something that led to the production of
four Gospels. For example, if it could be shown that someone,
somewhere, said to three people: 'Look, there are four zones
of the earth, four principal winds, and four living creatures; so
it is clear that there ought to be four Gospels: I shall write
one, you another, you another and you a fourth. Then there
will be the number that there should be.' Or an alternative
account would be if, when there were already three Gospels,
somebody said, 'This is wrong; Gospels should correspond in
number to the points of the compass and the faces of the
cherubim; I feel a call to be the fourth evangelist and make up
the number that is lacking.'
   To put it another way, we are interested in historical

theology, not in mystical theology; we want to know how the minds of human beings worked, not the mind of God. I remember, years ago, attending a celebration of the Orthodox liturgy in the chapel of a theological college. We noticed that the priest, at one point in the service, seemed to flap a cloth over the offerings on the altar, and we asked him afterwards why he did so. As I recollect his answer was, 'It is symbolic of the Holy Spirit, but actually it is to keep off the flies.' Did the flies come first, we wondered, and the symbolism later? Did the four Gospels happen for one reason, and was the number then explained in a different way?

What follows is one possible reconstruction of the events that led up to the acceptance of four Gospels by the Church – an event that had certainly happened by the time that Irenaeus was writing *Against Heresies*, or (probably) that Tatian was composing his *Diatessaron*. It must have been about the middle of the second century. This is only one possible reconstruction (what is sometimes called a 'scenario'); there may be others which would explain more of the facts, and some of them more satisfactorily. For what it is worth, here it is.

1. Somebody wrote what we call the Gospel according to Mark; he probably wrote it in the sixties or early seventies of the first century. We do not know where he wrote, but the subsequent history of the book requires the congregation for which it was written to have been in a place of some importance. It is not certain, and it may be in fact unlikely, that the author was an acquaintance of Peter, because it seems that there was more than one stage in the handing on of tradition between the eye-witnesses of the events and the writing of this book. It is not only that the book seems to contain legendary elements, such as voices from heaven, miraculous feedings, the lake-miracles and the cursing of the fig tree, but also the use of the expression 'the Son of Man' as a title is not, apparently, what one would expect from someone who had known Jesus and heard him speak in Aramaic.

The book was never referred to by any other title than According to Mark, or The Gospel according to Mark, as far as we know; and as there was no way of deducing this from the book's contents, it seems likely that it has always borne this name. But that does not necessarily tell us anything about who its author was.

As far as we know, no one had written anything similar to this book before. The only previous Christian writings of which we have certain knowledge were the letters of Paul – writings that carried their author's name, and had to, since they depended on his authority for dealing with the situations to which they were addressed. It is not so obvious that Mark's book was addressed to any particular situation; it is a narrative, and not manifestly part of a dispute.

One way to describe it would be to say that it was too good for its recipients. It made demands on its readers that were in excess of their capabilities. It operated on the basis of insiders and outsiders; it assumed that its readers would know how to interpret it; they had been given the secret of the kingdom of God. But this soon proved to be a false assumption.

The author's method was extraordinary. He wrote in an ironical way, so that the reader is expected to take nothing as it stands, but to realize the truth from its opposite. Think, for example, how each character or group of characters leaves the narrative: Judas, one of the twelve, has brought the party who will arrest Jesus, and he indicates which of those in Gethsemane is Jesus by kissing him; he is the only person in the whole book who is said to kiss Jesus. (In Mark's Greek, the same word, *phileō*, means both to love and to kiss.) The rest of the twelve, except Peter, then desert Jesus and run away, one of them preferring to go naked, rather than to be in the company of Christ. All of this has been foretold earlier in the evening in exact detail, as had also that which follows: Peter disowning Jesus three times, then remembering and weeping. This is the last we see of the male followers of Jesus. He himself is given nothing to say, apart from his declaration before the sanhedrin. He is called upon to prophesy, but the Spirit does not act as Jesus had promised that it would; it does not speak (through him); instead, it speaks through his opponents, the chief priests, Pilate, the soldiers, those who pass by; they, ironically, declare the truth about him without intending to do so; they mock him with the truth. Jesus therefore dies with his mind and his faith destroyed; his exit-line from the book is: My God, my God, why have you deserted me? Having disposed of all the males, Mark brings on the women, but not to prove that they are superior to the men; only to show that they are no better. One of them is referred to as Mary the mother of James and Joses; we are left to think that Mark means by this the mother of Jesus (6.3). The women fear, instead of believing; their fear is the cause of their disobedience to the young man's command, and the reason why they say nothing to anybody. So the book ends. It cannot go on, because there is no way that has yet been found of following Mark 16.8 with a further story that flows on from what has been said without hiatus, repetition or contradiction.

The end of the book was too good for the mind of the Church. It provoked two or three evangelists to improve on it, and two other writers to produce unsatisfactory endings – the longer and the shorter. It also caused some people to think that the original ending of the book had been lost. Only the scribes of *Codex Sinaiticus* and *Codex Vaticanus*, minuscule 304, and some ancient versions, left the book as Mark had finished it; all the rest asked the prosaic and improper question, What happened next? The question they should have asked was, What will happen next? Mark had given his readers the answer: The Son of Man will come to gather together his elect; so stay awake and be ready; you will see him when he comes to judge the world.

2. It was not just the end of Mark's Gospel that provoked others to write 'better' Gospels; it was also the apparent inability of Mark to answer so many questions: How are we to live? Is there a Christian community? Why are the Jews wrong? Is there no presence of Jesus, here and now? How can we go on, if all there is is waiting and enduring?

Sometime later – it may have been as long as twenty years

after Mark wrote – in another place (perhaps in Syria), one who knows Mark's book off by heart decides to deal with Mark's defects. He will enlarge it, revise it and censor it. He believes that he has the requisite charisma to do this. He adds five carefully organized speeches, each on its own topic: How to enter the kingdom of heaven; How to be an apostle; Parabolic teaching about faith and unbelief; How to be a member of the community; and finally, God's judgement on the Jews, on the Church and on the unbelievers. He also adds infancy stories, temptation stories and resurrection appearances. He revises the order of events in the first half of the book from what it was in Mark, so as to present Jesus as the one who has offered salvation to the Jews through his preaching, teaching and healing, and through the mission of the Twelve (sent to Israel only, to aggravate their guilt). He revises also Mark's suggestion that Jesus abolished the law; according to this later Gospel, Jesus fulfils the law by requiring a greater righteousness than that of the scribes and the Pharisees. And he omits certain features of Mark of which he did not approve: the use of saliva in healing; the open-shop attitude to the strange exorcist; the widow with the two coins; and the man who fled naked.

As far as we can judge, he had no idea that anyone would still use Mark after he had finished his revision of it and made it available; as R. H. Lightfoot used to say, he presumably tore up his copy of Mark and threw it into the wastepaper basket. He expected congregations that had copies of Mark to replace them with his own bigger and better book; he was not producing a supplement to Mark, he was supplanting it. And he almost succeeded. Scarcely anyone quoted Mark in the second century; no commentaries were written on Mark before the seventh century; there are only three surviving pieces of papyrus containing any part of Mark's text.

He never referred to Mark, his source, though he was totally dependent on him for his narrative from the baptism to the empty tomb. If you took out the Marcan material, Matthew's book would collapse into speeches that had no contexts. He gives his readers no idea that he is using 95 per cent of a previous writer's work, mainly in the same order and largely in the same words. He got away with it for nearly 1800 years, until he was rumbled by Lachmann.

He called himself Matthew, and unlike Mark he put his pseudonym into the narrative, and presumably on to the top of the book, or on the outside, or whatever it was you did. He did exactly the same as another pair of New Testament authors, probably rather later, but with the same effect: someone wrote Jude, and a later writer took over almost all of Jude and composed 2 Peter, making it look as though Jude was quoting him. The apostolic name is on the later document; the non-apostolic name is on the earlier document. The later writer does not refer to his source as his source. The later writer pretends he is the earlier, and makes it look as though he were the earlier. Just as, for centuries, people thought 2 Peter was prior to Jude, so also they thought that Matthew was earlier than Mark, his abbreviator and follower.

3. A third stage in the story involves another writer who certainly knows Mark's book and possibly Matthew's too. He takes Mark as his base, but he follows the procedure that Matthew had followed when dealing with Mark: like Matthew, he will add a genealogy, an annunciation, a birth-story and the coming of visitors to see the infant; like Matthew, he will expand the Baptist's preaching and describe three temptations of Jesus; like Matthew again, he will have a speech near the beginning of his book that will outline Jesus' teaching. But in each case, he will do what Matthew did in a slightly different way: the genealogy goes in the opposite direction, through a different line of David's descendants and stops with Adam, the son of God; the annunciation is not to Joseph but to Mary; the birth is in the same place, but because of a census, not because the family lived there; the visitors are shepherds, not magi; the temptations are in a different order, ending, like the book itself, in the temple; the sermon is not on a mountain, but on a level place.

Both Matthew and Luke add accounts of the appearances

of Jesus to his followers after the resurrection, but again there is a difference between them: the main appearance of Jesus in Matthew's book is in Galilee, whereas Luke's appearances are all within Jerusalem and the district nearby.

Luke makes a major decision which has important consequences: he decides to carry the story on beyond the resurrection and the appearances. He gives an account of the ascension which, as far as we know, had never been described in this way before. The Spirit comes to the Church in Jerusalem; only people who are in contact with Jerusalem and with those who have been there receive the Spirit. The offer of salvation to Jews continues throughout the second volume of the book, and is the subject of the final scene in Rome, whereas in Matthew, at the middle of the book, Jesus withdrew from the crowds and turned towards his disciples instead (13.36). Luke is less violent than Matthew in his attitude to unbelieving Jews, and there is less about hell in Luke than there was in Matthew, or about rewards as a motive for action. Luke's great gift is his ability to use stories to express the gospel: his parables are the ones we all know.

Unlike Matthew, Luke refers to his predecessors; he says there were many of them. In Acts, there is only one Christian person, apart from Ananias and Sapphira, who fails, and Luke tells us this about him twice: his name is Mark (13.13; 15.37f.). Is Luke commenting on his source, and is he, like Matthew, intending to make Mark's book redundant?

4. The final act is another case of what seems to be dissatisfaction with what was already available. The fourth evangelist may or may not have known any or all of the other three Gospels, but what is certain is that he is producing a book that expresses a different theology. We are not now waiting for the Son of Man to come from heaven, as in the final speech of Jesus (Mark 13; Matthew 23–25; Luke 21); there is no future that needs to be described; the great event has already happened, because Jesus came to his disciples on Easter Day, and breathed on them, and they received the Holy Spirit who is the presence of Christ with his disciples from the resurrec-

tion onwards. The believers are the mansions in which the Father and the Son dwell; they have eternal life; each is complete and has no need of others. There is no mention of church, or ministry; no need for sacraments; no ethics, no soteriology, no eschatology. The message of the book is personalized and individualized: the truth is Jesus, and he is in the believer and the believer is in him.

To present such a radical revision of the tradition, the writer invents a character we had never heard of before: the disciple whom Jesus loved. He is closer to Jesus than Peter had been; he does not disown Jesus when they are in the high priest's house; he remains by the cross and is designated by Jesus as the son of his mother.

The writer refers to other signs that are not in his book; but he says that they are not necessary; you need only his book in order to have eternal life. Like Matthew and Luke, John is aiming to supplant the previous writers.

The Fourth Gospel was not much used by the mainstream Christian writers till late in the second century, but some time in the middle of that century it became accepted along with the other three and in this way come into Tatian's *Diatessaron* and Irenaeus's fourfold Gospel.

It is interesting to note that the Gospel of Thomas does not present itself as a replacement of earlier Gospels; it is entirely a book of sayings of Jesus, and it seems to be meant to be understood as sayings of the risen Christ, the living Jesus. It has no narrative structure, such as Mark, Matthew, Luke and John all have; it does not therefore attempt to supplant any or all of them, but rather to supplement them. Whereas three of the Gospels that became canonical seem to have been meant by their authors to replace Mark, Thomas did not. And the surprising thing is that while they were unsuccessful in dislodging Mark (or any others of the four), but were accepted as part of the fourfold Gospel, Thomas was unsuccessful in its more modest aim of adding further sayings of Jesus to stand alongside the earlier traditions.

It is possible to draw five conclusions:

First, after Mark, the three next Gospels to be written were all produced through dissatisfaction with Mark, and perhaps with Matthew (in the case of Luke) and with all three, Mark, Matthew and Luke, in the case of John. Mark was the least used and the least valued. It is interesting that the Gospel which appeals to so many in the late twentieth century should have been so much disliked in its day. Its survival is evidence that it had the backing of an important congregation that was not willing to forego its traditional book for any of the attempted improvements and replacements.

Second, Gospels were originally written to stand on their own, and not alongside other similar books. A church had one Gospel and no more. The heretics who were one-Gospel men (whom Irenaeus mentions) were the conservatives, and the catholics, who had four, were the innovators. The fourfold Gospel was a new invention, and we do not know whose idea it was, or when or where it began.

Third, the account of how there came to be more than one Gospel in the Church is part of the story of Christian polemics, that goes back to the conflict between Paul and the church in Jerusalem and continues with the troubles of the late first-century churches (the Pastoral Epistles, the Apocalypse, etc.) and the controversies with gnosticism in the second century. Most Christian writing that has survived from this period was the result of intra-Christian rows. Had there been no controversies there would have been much less literature.

Fourth, Archbishop Trench pointed out that the two churches mentioned in the Apocalypse that had no internal conflicts were the two that were the weakest: Sardis and Laodicea. He suggested that the continuation of the truth depends in part on the existence of controversy. Dissatisfaction with Mark was necessary in order that other Gospels might be written. There must be heresies.

Finally, in the last fifty years or so we have seen the end of a period that began in the sixteenth century, and in which uniformity was thought to be an ideal for which the Church should strive: for example, uniformity in liturgy. Alternative service books now provide a vast number of alternative ways of performing the liturgy. Uniformity, in the sense of everyone saying the same words and acting according to the same rubrics, is no longer thought to be necessary or even desirable.

The four Gospels remind us that it was so in the second century also. They settled for four, not for one. It was a compromise, and we can appreciate it. Maybe we are the first people since the sixteenth century to understand it.

3

Preaching the Message of Jesus Now

THERE MUST HAVE BEEN a difference between what Jesus preached and what the apostles preached, if only because the one happened before the resurrection and the other after. The question to be considered is, granted that there was some difference, can we preach what Jesus preached, today?

First, only if we know what Jesus' message was. Immediately we run into problems, one of which has appeared quite recently. The usual view had been that there were certainly two sources (Mark and Q) and possibly two more (M and L); and that authentic sayings of Jesus might be found in all of them. However, it is now being argued[1] that Matthew had no source other than Mark, and that Luke had only Mark and Matthew; Q, L and M are all commentary. If this is true, then we shall only have Mark as the source for authentic sayings of Jesus. This thesis is still under discussion; therefore, I believe, the proper procedure is to adopt it, on the principle that when you are faced with alternative theories and cannot decide which is true, you should choose the more radical of the two, since it is always easier later on to move forwards than to retreat. (But if this seems too merely prudential, compare the advice of John of the Cross: 'Strive always to choose, not that which is easiest, but that which is most difficult; not that which gives most pleasure, but rather that which gives least . . .' *Ascent of Mount Carmel*, 1.13.6.) The question therefore now is, Can we discover what Jesus' message was, using only Marcan material?

It is frequently said that Mark tells us repeatedly *that* Jesus preached and taught, but not much about *what* he said; hence, presumably, the desire of Matthew and Luke to produce enlarged editions of Mark in which the content of the message could be set out more fully. However, the lack of content of Jesus' message in Mark is only apparent if you come to Mark with a previous knowledge of Matthew and Luke – which Mark's first readers did not possess. If on the other hand you read Mark straight through, and note the passages which indicate the content of Jesus' message, you end up with a long list of references, quite enough to give a clear indication of what Mark thought that Jesus had said. If you then apply to these passages the various tests for authenticity, you are still left with enough material to reconstruct an outline of Jesus' message. This material can be grouped under three heads: the situation; the call; the promise.

The situation

Jesus interpreted the situation in which he and his contemporaries found themselves in a different way from that in which other Jews of his time understood it. They said it was a time for fasting; he said it was not (2.19). He declared that Satan was tied and his house was being ransacked: that was the meaning of his exorcisms; God himself (the Holy Spirit) was at work (3.22–30). His teaching was, as people were noticing, unlike that of the doctors of the law; it was a new kind of teaching (1.21–8): for example, in marked contrast to other Jewish teachers, he seldom appealed to Scripture for authority. In many respects he dissociated what he said from what the religious authorities were saying: his teaching was new wine, and no one puts new wine into old wineskins (2.21f.). He deliberately caused offence by breaking the sabbath law (3.1–6; cf. 2.23–8) and told the doctors of the law who were Pharisees that he had not come to invite virtuous people, but sinners (2.17). He warned his disciples to be on their guard against the leaven of the Pharisees (8.15). Two particular instances of conflict with representatives of first-century Judaism were over what it is that defiles, and divorce (7.1–23;

10.1–9); he seems also to have disapproved of the worship in the temple at Jerusalem as it was conducted at that time (11.15–19) and to have foretold its destruction (13.1f; 14.58; 15.29).

The situation, according to Jesus, was that God was about to rule over the world (1.15; 9.1; 13.30; 14.25) and at such a time the laws of the Old Testament were out of date. But when the Pharisees asked him to demonstrate the truth of this assertion by providing a miracle to prove it, he refused (8.11–13).

The call

He refused to give a sign because his call was itself the sign; and his call was to repent, believe and follow him. Those who had ears to hear this invitation became his brothers and sisters (3.31–5); they would have eternal life in the age to come (10.28–31). It was the case with the disciples as with those who were healed: Your faith has cured you (5.34; 10.52). Every prop and support in this age must be abandoned (wealth, piety, domination over other people, self-security), and the disciple must live only by faith. Everything is possible to one who has faith (9.23); everything is possible for God (10.27); faith is therefore living out of the omnipotence of God. This is what is meant by becoming a child (9.33–7; 10.13–16).

The opposite to faith is fear: Do not be afraid; only have faith (5.36). If your trust is in anything less than God, then, because it is in that which can change and fail, your faith will be vulnerable to fear. But faith in God is not vulnerable in this way, because God is almighty; one of the reasons why the Sadducees, who said that there was no resurrection, were mistaken was because they did not know the power of God (12.18–27).

The call of Jesus was therefore an invitation to let go of everything except faith in the power of God, and to love him with all your heart, with all your soul, with all your mind and with all your strength. Those who did this would find that they were free to keep the second commandment, Love your neighbour as yourself (12.28–34); instead of using other people by lording it over them they would find it possible to act as servants and slaves to others (9.35; 10.41–5).

The promise

The message of Jesus was basically an invitation, and an invitation normally implies a forthcoming event to which you are invited. This future occasion, according to the message of Jesus, was the kingdom of God (1.15; 4.11, 26, 30; 9.1, 47; 10.23, 24, 25; 12.34; 14.25) or eternal life (9.43–5; 10.17–30) or being saved (8.35; 10.26; 13.13, 20); it would be preceded by the coming of the Son of Man in glory (8.38; 13.13, 24ff.). Jesus assured his hearers in four parables that this new age would indeed come: the sower – in spite of apparent failure, there will still be a harvest (4.1–8); the seed growing by itself – man does not know how it happens, but still there will be a harvest (4.26–9); the mustard seed – a great conclusion comes from a small beginning (4.30–2); the fig tree in spring – you can see the signs that the end is near (13.28–31). Then, when it comes, the poor will be rich, the first last and the last first (10.21, 31).

If we confine ourselves to Mark's Gospel as at present I believe we must, something like this seems to have been what Jesus said, or at least this seems to have been the fundamental outline of his message. We now have to ask the question, Can we preach what Jesus preached, today?

There is certainly one aspect which it is almost impossible to take over from the message of Jesus and preach again now, nineteen centuries later – namely, his expectation that the kingdom of God would come soon (1.15; 9.1; 12.34; 13.20; 14.62). We know that in fact it did not; and it is not altogether adequate or honest to say that it may even now come soon: *may* is not at all the same as *will*. We have to ask: Is the idea of the imminence of the end of this age essential to the message of Jesus? Is it so much the foundation of all that he said, that if we remove it all the rest will collapse?

If we think that it is essential, then we can say either that the whole movement which started with Jesus was a mistake, and that there is nothing in it; or that what is important in Christianity is not what Jesus said, but what he did, and that Christianity began not with the teaching of Jesus, but with the early preachers and Paul. Either of these is a possibility, but it should be said about the latter that it would certainly not be the traditional view: the Church has always paid greater respect to the Gospels than to the Epistles (in the eucharist, for example), and has appealed behind the apostle to the words of the Lord in the days of his flesh.

But is the imminence of the end essential to the message of Jesus? How soon is imminent? If Jesus said, The present generation will live to see it all (13.30), would it make any real difference to the truth of what he had said if the end had come after one of his contemporaries had died, or a year after the death of the last of them? And if one year would not have mattered, why nineteen hundred or nineteen million?

If it is true that Jesus taught in all honesty the way of life that God requires (12.14) while expecting this age to end soon, we can still learn from his teaching the way of life that God requires even if we do not expect the end to come soon. There are certain matters which we should all agree would be right (or wrong) whether we thought that the world was about to end tomorrow or to continue for two thousand million years (love, honesty, justice, for example) – though it must be admitted that there are also certain matters on which we should hold one opinion if we believed in the imminent end of the world and another if we did not (using up the mineral resources of the planet, pollution, planting trees, life-insurance, for example).

The fact of the matter probably is that one of the situations in which you see what life is about with greater clarity is when you believe that you are near to the edge of it: apocalyptic, like hanging, concentrates the mind wonderfully. Jesus, and many other first-century Jews, thought that God was about to intervene finally in the history of the world; what he preached on the basis of this assumption was very different from what they taught. The question is, Was he right?

Those who believe that he was right might perhaps want to say what it is they believe in some such way as this: If I find myself living as though life was a struggle, with obstacles to be overcome and threats to be warded off, then I am mistaken; life is not like that. There are no threats or obstacles, except those which I create in my own imagination. And the cause of my imagining these things is the manner in which I direct my love and attention: I make myself the centre of my existence and live for myself. Had I the courage to disestablish myself and live for whatever is not myself, I should certainly suffer, but I should not be afraid.

It is scarcely necessary to add that such a view of life – when it came to concrete and specific occasions – would seem impractical and insane. Mark tells us that people were saying of Jesus that he was out of his mind; and that the doctors of the law said, He is possessed by Beelzebul (3.21–2). The message of Jesus, if we could hear it, would always appear to us as a kind of madness; if it did not, that would mean that we had not heard it aright.

Can we preach what Jesus preached today? Yes, if by a miracle we can believe that what he said is true. It need not follow that we always preach only the message of Jesus: there is variety in the New Testament (contrast Paul with James) and there can and perhaps should be variety in our preaching too. However, it may be that today is one of those periods of history in which what is needed most is the message of Jesus. Years ago, Professor C. F. Evans used to say (but I am not sure whether he would still wish to be held to it) that the Bible is like a series of time-bombs which go off, one after another. To elaborate this – and it may be a gross oversimplification – it seems as though there have been Paul-bombs and Jesus-bombs: Marcion, Augustine, Luther, Calvin, Wesley and Barth were Paul-bombs; in them the Pauline teaching went off and started a new movement in the Church. Antony of Egypt, Francis of Assisi and Charles de Foucauld were Jesus-bombs; in them the message of Jesus came alive once more.

All the indications are that the present is ripe for a Jesus-bomb, rather than for one of Paul's. And the counterfeits and inferior copies which arc readily available on the market under this label make it all the more important that we find and explode the genuine article.

Note

1   By M. D. Goulder, in 'The Composition of the Lord's Prayer', *Journal of Theological Studies* n.s. 14, pp. 32ff.; 'Characteristics of the Parables in the Several Gospels', *Journal of Theological Studies* n.s. 19, pp. 51ff.; and in *Midrash and Lection in Matthew: The Speaker's Lectures in Biblical Studies, 1969–71* (London: SPCK, 1974).

4

John of the Cross and the Gospel According to Mark

A STRANGE PAIR TO BRING TOGETHER, you might think – John of the Cross and the author of the Gospel according to Mark. John lived in Spain in the sixteenth century, and never left it; he was born in 1542 and died in 1591; Henry VIII was king of England when he was born; the first English Prayer Book of 1549 came out when he was seven (and he almost certainly knew nothing about it, then or later); William Shakespeare was born when he was 18; the Armada was defeated when he was 46, and he died just before his fiftieth birthday, when Queen Elizabeth I still had twelve more years on the English throne.

All we know about Mark is what we can gather from one small book written in Greek, somewhere in the Roman empire, perhaps around the year AD 70. John (by whom is meant John of the Cross throughout this chapter; the Gospel of that name will be referred to as the Fourth Gospel) – John was a poet, who wrote in Spanish, and composed commentaries on his own poems which fill three volumes in the English translation of E. Allison Peers (1934, reprinted 1943); Mark was a storyteller, who used stories as his way of proclaiming the good news. John was trained in scholastic philosophy and theology, and owed much to traditions of devotion that went back, by way of Bernard of Clairvaux and Pseudo-Dionysius, to the Song of Songs in the Old Testament interpreted allegorically; Mark's immediate background was probably the teaching of Paul and, behind that, Jewish apocalyptic, and ultimately a different Old Testament book (the last to be written), Daniel. Of course John knew Mark's

Gospel: he had only two books in his cell, we are told, and one of them was the Bible (which in any case, they say, he knew off by heart); he knew Mark's Gospel, but he does not often quote Mark's Gospel: according to the index in Allison Peers' *Complete Works* the figures are: Matthew 65 times; Mark 3 times; Luke 54 times; the Fourth Gospel 85 times. So the Fourth Gospel was the one he quoted most frequently, and Mark's the one he quoted least frequently, and by a long way: 85:3. But as we shall see later, there is one particular passage in one of John's works in which he explicitly mentions a chapter in Mark, and draws his readers' attention to it with great emphasis.

History was kinder to John than to Mark; John was beatified within a century of his death (in 1675), canonized fifty years later (in 1726), and declared a Doctor of the Church (in 1926). Mark, on the other hand, was regarded as the follower and abbreviator of Matthew; no commentary was written on him before the seventh century, unless one counts a catena by Victor of Antioch in the fifth century; but there is no commentary on Mark by Origen, Chrysostom, Jerome or Augustine. Interest in Mark began only in the first half of the nineteenth century, when it was suggested that it might be the oldest of the four Gospels and one of their sources; and it was not until the beginning of the twentieth century that anyone thought of Mark as more than a collector and editor of other people's reminiscences. Then, in 1901, for the first time, he was treated as a real author, a writer of profound thought and skill.

So the question is, why bring two such different writers together, and try to talk about both of them in one chapter?

Suppose someone comes along and says to you: I think I get the point of Matthew; it's all about impossible commands that are made possible because Christ is present with his disciples till the end of the world. I think I get the point of Luke; it's all about Christ the friend of sinners, and his offer of repentance and forgiveness; the parables are the main thing in Luke. I think I get the point of the Fourth Gospel; it's all about eternal life, and how you can have it now; this life is in God's Son; if you have the Son, you have life. But try as I may, I cannot see what the point of Mark is. I know he has more miracles per page than any of the other three; I know he hates the disciples; I know there is a problem about the end of the Gospel. In Mark, Jesus is remote; people are afraid of him and daren't ask him questions, and are always wrong whatever they say or do; and his own exit-line is My God, my God, why have you abandoned me? We never see him again after that. Tell me what to do, so that I can make some sort of sense of the Gospel according to Mark, because it does not seem to me much of a Gospel, a book of good news, at all.

If someone said that, then the answer would be – and it's obviously impractical and of no use to the majority of those who might conceivably ask such a question about Mark, if indeed anyone would – but the answer is: Read John of the Cross, and then you will see the point of Mark's Gospel. Take John as the prologue to Mark. You will understand and appreciate Mark, if your taste is educated through reading John.

To say that might provoke the comment: Aren't you taking a sledgehammer to crack a nut? Yes, indeed: but what a sledgehammer! and what a nut!

How would reading John of the Cross help me to understand the Gospel according to Mark? – that is the question; where shall we begin? At the end. Both writers believe in a future of the purest joy and happiness. Both of them are writing with the purpose of telling their readers or hearers how to live now, in order to arrive at that future, reach the goal and participate in the bliss. Both writers are controlled and dominated by hope: the hope of glory; the hope of salvation; seeing God and being united with him.

There are differences in the way they write about it; but we need not, must not, be put off by that. What they have in common is far more important than how they differ. It would be superficial and far too slick to say, Mark is looking forward to the kingdom of God on earth; John is looking forward to the union of the soul with God in heaven. Mark's thinking is corporate, and includes the renewal of all creation; John's is individualistic, and shows no interest in the redemption of the natural order. Much of this may be true, but it is largely irrelevant and partly not even true. Mark, for example, like John, uses the marriage metaphor, though in a different way: Christ is the bridegroom who will be taken away (2.19f.) but will come again (13.26f.). According to Mark, the root of uncleanness is in the heart of the individual; there is a sort of individualism in Mark, just as there is in John:

> From inside, from the human heart,
> come evil thoughts, acts of fornication,
> theft, murder, adultery, greed, and malice;
> fraud, indecency, envy, slander,
> arrogance, and folly; all these evil things
> come from within, and they are what defile a person.
> (Mark 7.20ff.)

Moreover, Mark uses stories of miraculous healing to express the good news of salvation, and he does so more frequently than any of the other three evangelists; there are thirteen individuals healed, whose cures are described in detail. The good news that 'Your faith has saved you' is put before us by means of accounts of sick and crippled individuals being made well. There is no fundamental difference here between Mark and John: both are writing about a future of indescribable joy; for both, the present is overshadowed by the future that is to come. (On the day I wrote this (20 April 1992) *The Times* carried an obituary of the late Frankie Howerd, which ended like this: Once asked for his favourite memory, he replied: 'It hasn't happened yet.' Mark and John of the Cross would both have enjoyed that; in fact, it is almost a quotation from John.) Commentating on the lines in *The Spiritual Canticle*:

> There wouldst thou show me
> That which my soul desired

John writes:

> This desire is the equality of love which the soul ever desires,
> both naturally and supernaturally, because the lover cannot be
> satisfied if he feels not that he loves as much as he is loved. And
> as the soul sees the truth of the vastness of the love wherewith
> God loves her, she desires not to love him less loftily and per-
> fectly, to which end she desires present transformation,
> because the soul cannot reach this equality and completeness
> of love save by the total transformation of her will in that of
> God, wherein the two wills are united after such manner that
> they become one . . . She will love Him even as much as she is
> loved by God. (*Complete Works*, ii. 172f.)

John shows us how what we long for, what our future is, is
union with God in love; like bride and bridegroom, as in the
Song of Songs, a book he treasured; when he was dying, he
asked for it to be read to him: Read me some verses from the
Song of Songs, he begged. The prior complied (E. A. Peers,
Spirit of Flame, p. 80).

Another quotation from *The Spiritual Canticle* makes the
same point: that our longing is for union with God. John is
commenting on the line in his poem:

> And let us go to see ourselves in thy beauty.

He says:

> Which signifies: Let us so act that, by means of this exercise of
> love aforementioned, we may come to see ourselves in Thy
> beauty: that is, that we may be alike in beauty, and that Thy
> beauty may be such that, when one of us looks at the other,
> each may be like to Thee in Thy beauty, and may see himself in
> Thy beauty, which will be the transforming of me in Thy
> beauty; and thus I shall see Thee in Thy beauty and Thou wilt
> see me in Thy beauty; and Thou wilt see Thyself in me in Thy
> beauty, and I shall see myself in Thee in Thy beauty; and thus I
> may be like to Thee in Thy beauty and Thou mayest be like to

me in Thy beauty, and my beauty may be Thy beauty, and Thy beauty my beauty; and I shall be Thou in Thy beauty and Thou wilt be I in Thy beauty, because Thy beauty itself will be my beauty. (*Complete Works*, ii. 164)

All of John's writing is controlled by hope of God and longing for union with him in love. Mark, too, is about the future, and the key term that he uses to express it is the kingdom of God. He has it fourteen times in his Gospel, thirteen of which are in the direct speech of Jesus. It comes, for example, in the first words of Jesus in the book:

The time is fulfilled and the kingdom of God has come near. (1.15)

Again, at the end, just before they sing the Passover hymn and leave the house to go to Gethsemane, Jesus takes an oath of abstinence from wine until the kingdom comes:

Truly I tell you: never again shall I drink from the fruit of the vine until that day when I drink it new in the kingdom of God. (14.25)

It is not the Song of Songs for Mark, but Daniel that he starts from: four world empires to be followed by God's direct rule on the earth. In Daniel 2, the image of gold, silver, bronze, iron and clay (that is, Babylon, Medea, Persia, Greece) will be totally destroyed by a stone that will fill the whole world; God's rule will abolish and replace all human politics. Then again, in chapter 7, which is the chiastic pair to chapter 2, the four beasts are also the four empires, and they will be replaced by God's rule, symbolized now not by a stone but by one who is like a human being. Mark is looking forward to that time, and his Gospel is rich in allusions to Daniel. Jesus, he believes, will come as the Son of Man whom Daniel had seen, and he will send his angels to gather the elect from the four winds into his kingdom. The tree in which the birds roost (Mark 4.32) refers back to the tree that Daniel had described (4.12); it is the symbol of kingly power, which God gives and takes back, in order that, in the end, he may exercise it himself.

That will be the time of salvation. Mark sets it before us in his eighteen miracle-stories: instead of demons and madness, there will be sanity; instead of sickness, health; instead of uncleanness, holiness; instead of defects, activity; instead of guilt, forgiveness; instead of sea and storms, peace; instead of hunger, plenty; instead of barrenness, fruitfulness; instead of death, life.

The miracles in Mark point to the life that there will be on the earth when God begins to rule; even more important than the miracles is the first commandment of the law:

> The first is, Hear, O Israel: the Lord our God is the one Lord and you must love the Lord your God with all your heart, with all your soul, with all your mind, and with all your strength. (12.29)

When the scribe agrees with him, Jesus says:

> You are not far from the kingdom of God. (12.34)

Whatever that difficult saying means precisely, it must include the idea that to love God and to enter his kingdom are closely associated.

We can see Mark's longing for the future in the one and only long, continuous speech of Jesus that he includes, in chapter 13; it is all about what must happen (13.7, a phrase from Daniel 2.28) before the Son of Man comes and that new age begins, in which we shall be as angels 12.25), resurrected, healed, set free from all that hinders us now from loving God as we should. We shall be perfect in love. Mark's book ends with the promise that it shall be so:

> Tell his disciples, and Peter,
> He is going ahead of you into Galilee,
> there you will see him, as he told you. (16.7)

He had told them that they would see the kingdom of God come in power (9.1); and that they would see the Son of Man coming in the clouds (13.26; 14.62). The future is the time for seeing, and for loving what we shall see. Like Bartimaeus, we shall recover our sight and we shall follow Jesus to Jerusalem and to Galilee; we shall be saved.

John and Mark, then, are both writing about something that is in the future, and is to control all our decisions and choices in the present.

John believes that our future is union with God in love, and the figure that he frequently uses to describe it is marriage. Moreover, because marriage is an exclusive relationship, John teaches with vigorous and systematic ruthlessness that there must be no other object in our affections than God alone. To get rid of our other loves, we shall have to enter the Dark Night, and this will involve us in mortification, the annihilation of self. Here is one of his much-quoted passages on mortification:

> Strive always to choose, not that which is easiest but that which is most difficult;
> Not that which is most delectable, but that which is most unpleasing;
> Not that which gives most pleasure, but rather that which gives least;
> Not that which is restful, but that which is wearisome;
> Not that which gives most consolation, but rather that which makes disconsolate;
> Not that which is greatest, but that which is least;
> Not that which is loftiest, and most precious, but that which is lowest and most despised;
> Not that which is a desire for anything, but that which is a desire for nothing;
> Strive not to go about seeking the best of temporal things, but the worst.
> Strive thus to desire to enter into complete detachment and emptiness and poverty, with respect to that which is in the world, for Christ's sake. (*Complete Works*, i. 61)

It is shortly after this passage, which comes at the end of Book I of the *Ascent of Mount Carmel*, that John makes his one and, as far as I can see, only explicit reference to Mark's Gospel. It is in Book II of the *Ascent*, chapter 7, paragraph 4:

> It is clearly seen that the soul must not only be disencumbered from that which belongs to the creatures, but likewise, as it travels, must be annihilated and detached from all that belongs to its spirit. Wherefore Our Lord instructing us and leading us into this road gave, in the eighth chapter of S. Mark, that wonderful teaching of which I think it may almost be said that, the more necessary it is for spiritual persons, the less it is practised by them. As this teaching is so important and so much to our purpose, I shall reproduce it here in full, and expound it according to its real and spiritual sense.

John then writes out Mark 8, verses 34 and 35, in Latin, and then provides the Spanish translation, of which this is the English:

> If any man will follow My road, let him deny himself and take up his cross and follow Me. For he that will save his soul shall lose it; but he that loses it for My sake, shall gain it. (*Complete Works*, i. 88f.)

The strange and surprising thing about this passage in John is the reference to Mark's Gospel. Until the nineteenth century and the theory that Mark was the earliest Gospel, writers usually quoted from Matthew, if the passage they wanted to refer to was in Matthew; and John normally follows this practice. Hence his infrequent quotations from Mark. The two verses that he quotes here, Mark 8.34, 35, are also in Matthew, in virtually identical words: Matthew 16.24, 25. The question therefore arises, Why did John refer to Mark 8 at this point in the *Ascent* when he could equally well have referred to Matthew 16? The only answer I can think of – and there is no way of testing it – is that he had noticed the repeated emphasis in Mark 8 to 12 on disowning yourself, if you want to be a follower of Christ.

In John, it is the Ascent of Mount Carmel; and he tells us what that means: union of the soul with God (*Complete Works*, i. 9). In Mark, chapters 8 to 12 are also on ascent, but to Jerusalem (10.33). To be followers of Jesus on this road they must renounce self, destroy their lives, lose the world. They must be like the children whom Jesus hugs, once in chapter 9 and again in chapter 10; because children have no property or status; they are nobodies; they do not count; they are no better than slaves, Paul had said (Galatians 4.1). Mark's account of self-annihilation is as ruthless as John's; it includes cutting off your hand or your foot and tearing out your eye (9.43–8). Mark has a saying of Jesus so severe and devastating that both Matthew and Luke omit it:

Everyone will be salted with fire. (9.49)

It is a parody of an instruction in Leviticus (2.13):

Every offering of sacrifice is to be salted with salt.

Under the old covenant, sacrifices were made acceptable to God by adding salt; under the new covenant, the worshippers are the sacrifice, and the way in which they are made acceptable to God is by fire; that is, by destruction. Mark puts the rich man immediately after the second passage about children, and the lesson is the same; the man asks what he must do to inherit eternal life. He is somebody who has everything, including having kept all the commandments since he was a child. But a rich man, by definition, lacks one thing, and it happens to be the only thing that matters: poverty; so:

Go, sell everything you have . . . follow me (10.21)

Mark returns to the theme in the final story before chapter 13 and the passion and resurrection in 14–16; it is the story of the widow in the temple, with two tiny coins, and she puts both of them into the chest. She is the model for a disciple; Mark says it three times, because it is true:

> She has put in everything (*panta*)
> as much as she had (*hosa eichen*)
> the whole of her life (*holon ton bion autēs*).

Mark's story tells us nothing about what she did next: How did she pay the rent? How did she buy her food? Was she acting prudently? Did somebody have to look after her? Mark tells us none of these things because he is not interested in that sort of problem. His stories are not realistic. He only wants us to think one thing: Love for God cannot coexist with any other sort of love; it is exclusive in its demands; it is like marriage; there is no place for a bit on the side; all your heart, all your soul, all your mind, all your strength – and all your money, too.

Probably the characteristic of both John and Mark that is most offensive, particularly in an affluent society, is their negative attitudes. Here, for example, is John:

> In order to come to union with the wisdom of God, the soul has to proceed rather by unknowing than by knowing; and all the dominion and liberty of the world, compared with the liberty and dominion of the spirit of God, is the most abject slavery, affliction and captivity. Wherefore the soul that is enamoured of prelacy, or of any other such office, and longs for liberty of desire, is considered and treated, in the sight of God, not as a son, but as a base slave and captive, since it has not been willing to accept His holy doctrine, wherein He teaches us that he who would be greater must be less, and he who would be less must be greater. (*Complete Works*, i. 27)

John obviously has in mind the story of the request of James and John for chief seats in glory; it is from Mark 10 (he refers to it again, elsewhere):

Whoever wants to be great must be your servant,
and whoever wants to be first must be the slave of all. (10.43f.)

It is not only ecclesiastical ambition that John is against –
wanting to be a canon; he warns his readers against any devo-
tional feelings, or hearing voices, or seeing visions, or any
physical experience at all. The union that we are made for is
union with God and God cannot be experienced physically,
because he is not a material object. Union is to be with God,
therefore nothing must be allowed to get in the way of it – no
attachment of any kind; particularly no religious attachments,
because they are the most insidious. This is the area in which
John appears to us most negative.

Of course it is a mistake to think of this as negative; we only
need to look at what he is saying in a different way – and he
provides the simile that we need. Sunlight strikes a pane of
glass: if the glass is clean, the ray goes straight through the
glass, as if it were not there. No one would think of criticizing
window-cleaners as people whose work was purely negative;
nor is John to be criticized in this respect.

Mark is superbly negative in the same way. The coming
rule of God on the earth will abolish all kinds of authority –
human and demonic. The miracle-story that he chooses to
put first is the one in which the demoniac in the synagogue
cries out:

You have come to destroy us. (1.24)

He speaks the truth: God's rule will destroy demons and
synagogues, Satan, the law and the temple. Jesus will rebuild
a new temple in which there will be no more offerings and
sacrifices, as the scribe had half-expected (12.33). Not even
religion will get between us and God.

The demons in Mark know who Jesus is, but he silences
them. John shows us why: the Devil is a great deceiver. The
important truth about Jesus, as Mark sees it, is not who he is
– Christ, Son of God, Son of Man, Holy One of God – that's
what demons know; but what he does; and what he does is, he

dies. He dies, abandoned by God. That is all we see in Mark: he will not be seen again until the final union in the age to come.

The last two chapters of Mark are rich in irony. For example, the women in chapter 16 come in unbelief to anoint a corpse on the very day he told them he would rise; and talk about moving a stone already moved. They refuse to believe, and instead they are afraid: these are the only alternatives (5.36). In the past, people had spoken, when told to be silent; now they are silent, when they are told to speak.

But it is the paragraph before this (15.42–7) where the irony is stronger and the humour even blacker. Joseph of Arimathea also is longing for the kingdom of God, like Jesus, who had spoken about it thirteen times, and died with the title King of the Jews on his cross. Joseph asks for the body (*sōma*) of Jesus, and Pilate makes a present of the carcass (*ptōma*): the man who longed for life found himself landed with a dead corpse. Life is through death; light is through darkness. The story of the burial epitomizes the teaching of Mark's book and illustrates the main theme in John of the Cross:

> In order to arrive at having pleasure in everything,
> Desire to have pleasure in nothing (*Complete Works*, i. 62)

Compare two passages, one from each. First, from *The Dark Night of the Soul*, where John is commenting on the line,

> By the secret ladder, disguised.

The secret ladder, he says, is dark contemplation by which the soul goes forth to union with God:

> It is like one who sees something never seen before,
> whereof he has not even seen the like;
> although he might understand its
> nature and have experience of it, he
> would be unable to give it a name, or say

41

what it is, however much he tried to do so,
and this in spite of its being a thing which
he had perceived with his senses. How much
less, then, could he describe a thing that has
not entered through the senses! For the language
of God has this characteristic that, since it
is very intimate and spiritual in its relations
with the soul, it transcends every sense and at
once makes all harmony and capacity of the
outward and inward senses to cease and be dumb.
(*Complete Works*, i. 457)

We come to God by this secret ladder which is our inability
to describe him, to give him a name.

Compare this with Mark 13 verses 5 to 37, the final speech
of Jesus; and notice first the high rate of use of negatives: *ou,
mē, oude, oupo̅,* etc. In 33 verses there are 27 instances of some
form of the negative.

Let no one mislead you. People will say, I am he; do not believe
them. There will be national and natural disasters; that is only
the beginning . . . There will be persecution; do not worry what
to say . . . Do not try to take anything with you; do not fetch
anything from house or field . . . There will be false messiahs
and false prophets; do not believe them. They will do miracles;
that is only another form of deception. Hang on until all the
lights of the created order have gone out:

The sun darkened
the moon not giving its light
the stars falling from the sky.

When it is totally dark, you will see the Son of man coming,
and you will see him because his clothes will shine with
dazzling whiteness, just as the three disciples had seen him at
the transfiguration.

Mark provides no description of the life of the new age; he makes no attempt to describe the new heaven, the new earth, or the city that will come down from God. Mark knows, as John knew later, that the language of God makes us dumb. After 20 verses of preparation for the end, describing the waiting, warning us against being misled, there are only two verses describing the coming and the gathering. The reader of John is not surprised by the silence of Mark.

To sum up and conclude: this chapter has been about one idea, and only one. It contains a modest and practical suggestion. If you could not find the point of Mark's Gospel, it might help if you read John of the Cross. Although he was living in sixteenth-century Spain, far removed from Mark in time and probably in space, his teaching illuminates Mark's Gospel, written in the Roman empire in the first century. To put it at its lowest, there is a similarity of thought between these two great Christian writers. They both believed that God is beyond our experience; they are both saying, It is not this; don't hang on to anything; the arrows are beyond you. Or, if that is to say too much, could we put it like this: might it be that if we came to Mark from John of the Cross we should find one way of reading that Gospel that would yield a sort of Christian sense? No doubt there are endless ways of reading Mark's text; John gives us one, and it is one that has proved itself to many, over many centuries.

5

Mark's Gospel: The Oldest and the Best?

W E CAN, I HOPE, assume that people will go on reading
Gospels in the future. They've done so for 20 centuries
so why should they stop now? But they will have their own
way of reading the Gospels – a way that is different from the
way people have read them in the past. It is a way of reading
the Gospels that seems to be emerging for use in the twenty-
first century that I want to talk about, in particular in relation
to Mark's Gospel. I can illustrate this from my own forebears.

My grandfather was an evangelical clergyman who lived in
the north of England and who died in the year 1900. He
would have known absolutely nothing about what I'm going
to talk about because it had not come out in 1900. He had
four sons who survived infancy who all became Anglican
evangelical clergymen. The youngest was my father who died
in 1934; he was the last to die, and neither he nor they would
have known almost anything at all about what I'm going to
talk about. So what we have is something that is fairly recent,
and had not been thought about in the past.

The two dates are interesting. In 1901 a book came out by
a German writer called Wrede, *The Messianic Secret*, that was
moving towards the way we think nowadays. But my grandfather died the year before. And in 1934 a book came out by
an American professor from Harvard University called James
Hardy Ropes, a little book entitled *The Synoptic Gospels*. That
announced what is now very popular, a new approach to the
Gospels, but my father wouldn't have read it – it was the year
he died.

You can see the difference between how they used the

Gospels in the earlier centuries, especially in the nineteenth and the early part of the twentieth century, and the way we think now, if you contrast what I'm going to say with someone like Bishop Westcott, Bishop of Durham. In 1881, in the commentary on St John's Gospel, the passage on 'The Seven Words from the Cross' explains how all seven were said by Jesus and works out the order in which they must have been spoken. Gospels up to the middle of the twentieth century were being used to try to find out what happened. People were not so interested in the authors; they were trying to get behind the authors to what happened. They were more interested in the historical Jesus than in the evangelists. Now, what we are interested in is how evangelists work, what they are doing, how they tell us what the gospel is.

Certainly, my grandfather and my uncles and my father would not have been surprised to hear that someone was talking about Mark as the oldest Gospel. That had been proposed in 1835, so it was old news by then. Karl Lachmann in Germany was the first person, I believe, to argue for Mark as the oldest Gospel. Until then people had thought Matthew was the oldest Gospel, which is what Augustine in North Africa had said in the fifth century. Protestants took up this idea of Mark being the oldest Gospel from 1835 onwards more and more. Roman Catholics on the other hand were not allowed to think that until 1962 – the Second Vatican Council; now for Roman Catholics there is no problem about accepting Mark as the oldest Gospel.

What are the reasons for thinking Mark is the oldest? One is that it is the shortest of the four. There is a general rule of thumb that shorter texts are older than longer texts when they are similar to one another, especially in the case of religious texts, because religion tends to be conservative and preserve things rather than abbreviate or get rid of things. So it was easier to think that the shorter text was the earlier one. It also became clear to some people that you could explain the development from Mark to Matthew and Luke and John more easily than try to explain the order in any other direction. One must remember that from AD 400 or so onwards everyone had thought that Mark was an abbreviation of Matthew. There was a major change in 1835.

My father and his brothers and his father would not have had any problem with the priority of Mark, but how could we say that Mark is the best of the four Gospels? Perhaps it was an unfortunate thing to suggest but what I meant by best was best for us and best for some years to come – more suited to our needs and the needs of the twenty-first century as I imagine them. To suggest this is certainly a change of under-standing about Mark, because it used to be the one that was used least. In the Anglican tradition, in the Prayer Book that was written by Archbishop Cranmer in 1549 and then revised at various dates until 1662, there are 53 Sunday Gospels, and of those 53, 20 are from Matthew and only two from Mark. So Mark was comparatively ignored between 1549 and 1662, and this went on until a revision in 1980 in the Church of England, when John became the most popular one and Mark was still bottom in popularity ratings. The Common Lec-tionary that a lot of people are now using has solved the problem by having a year for Matthew, a year for Mark and a year for Luke. The point that is made by that way of reading Gospels is that each Gospel should be read on its own, not cut up into little bits which are shuffled and then dealt out in a different order. That is no way to read a book. Almost all authors expect their books to be read from the beginning to the end; whether that happens or not, still people expect that, especially if the book is one that has a story-line in it, it is meant to be read from beginning to end. Not all books, however, should be read from beginning to end. You would not read railway timetables from beginning to end or tele-phone directories.

Nowadays we have got the idea that Mark is a real book, that it had a real author who had real purposes and a plan, who wanted to achieve a certain effect, so that when people read his book they would be in a position that was different from the one they were in before. This way of seeing Mark's book as a real book to be interested in started with Wrede in 1901. It was encouraged by J. M. Creed in Cambridge in the

1930s, then Ropes in Harvard in 1934, and then Robert Henry Lightfoot, a professor at Oxford, whose student I had the good luck to be. He gave the Bampton Lectures in 1934, which were published in 1935. And then Austin Farrer, in a book published in 1951 called *A Study in St Mark*. From then on an unstoppable stream of books has come out on Mark. All this would have surprised people living before 1934 because they thought: Mark is written in very poor Greek, so therefore, he must have been a man who had no good ideas. He was simply a collector of paragraphs. He wrote what he could remember Peter had said, in the wrong order, and what they were interested in was nothing to do with Mark, but possibly with Peter, and more with simply what happened. That was the old way.

Now, why might anyone say that Mark is the best for us? The answer I think is because it communicates the gospel, the good news, more effectively than any of the other three. To see this it is a help to go back to St Paul, who wrote before Mark, and lived and died before Mark. Paul, writing to the Corinthians, says: 'The cross is sheer folly to some. God chose the folly of the gospel to save those who had faith. We proclaim Christ nailed to the cross, an offence to Jews, folly to gentiles.' And he said, further on in 1 Corinthians, 'We are fools for Christ's sake.'

This gives us an entry into understanding Mark's book. It is a foolish book. Give it to anybody who doesn't know anything else about it, just give it to someone to read as it stands, and they will say, 'What an extraordinarily sad story, and what a useless sort of story. It has no point, it doesn't get anywhere, it's just a series of disasters from beginning to end.' The family of Jesus, in chapter 3 of Mark, come to arrest him because they say he's mad. And he says of his mother, 'She's not my mother', and of his brothers and sisters, 'they're not my brothers and sisters'. Scribes come from Jerusalem, also in chapter 3, and they say, 'He's possessed by the ruler of the demons.' A crowd, in chapter 4, are outsiders, and the comment about them is that they look and look but see nothing, they listen and listen but understand nothing, they do not turn to God and they are not forgiven. The chief priests, elders and scribes condemn Jesus to death as a blasphemer. The crowd in Jerusalem prefers Barabbas, a murderer. Pilate, the Roman governor, agrees, in order to satisfy the mob, that Jesus should be put to death.

The disciples, surely they will have some understanding and they will remain loyal to him – they have the secret of the kingdom of God? No they don't. Mark portrays the disciples as failures, almost from the beginning of the book to the end. Every time it says they are 'afraid' it means they lack under-standing; 'amazed', 'astonished' means they don't believe. They run away when Jesus is arrested, one of them leaving his clothes behind, preferring nakedness to being with Jesus. And you have to remember here that these Hebrews hated the idea of nakedness. Hebrews hated taking their clothes off – see the story of Noah drunk after the flood. Jesus' final words in Mark's book are the unanswered question, 'My God, my God, why have you forsaken me?' (Mark 15.34).

The women who come after the disciples have fled are no better than the men. In spite of the predictions that he would be raised after three days, they come to anoint a corpse on the very day that he has predicted resurrection. We are told what their thoughts are: they are worried about moving the stone. They are wrong about the stone because it has been moved already, and they're wrong about the body because Jesus has been raised, he is not there. The young man in white tells them, 'You'll see him in Galilee as he told you.' What had he told them? He told them they would see the Son of Man coming in glory. But like the men, the women flee in fear and trembling and say nothing to anybody.

So nobody knows about the resurrection. Except the young man in white and the omniscient writer of the book. This is where Mark's text stopped. This is one of the great discoveries of the twentieth century – that Mark stopped in chapter 16, at verse 8. In the British Library's *Codex Sinaiticus* Mark stops at 16.8. The last words are, 'They said nothing to anybody because they were afraid.' In *Codex Vaticanus*, in the Vatican Library, Mark also stops there. If you go to Mount Sinai and ask for the *Sinaitic Syriac*, you will find that that stops at 16.8. There are various other ancient versions of the translations of the Scriptures, in Sahidic and Armenian, and some of them stop there, and some of the Fathers knew manuscripts that stopped at that point. There never was a lost ending of Mark. Mark never intended to go on beyond this point. You can see this if you take Mark 16.1–8 and then try to write the next paragraph without hesitation, deviation, contradiction or repetition. Mark has painted himself into a corner and cannot go on. If the disciples are to go to Galilee to see him, then someone has got to tell them to go to Galilee. The women, it is said, will not; they said nothing to anybody because they were afraid. Who can get the message from the tomb to the disciples? You would have to bring someone on. And who knows where the grave is, other than the women? This is where Mark meant to stop.

The only people who come out of Mark's story with any sort of success or honour, or gain our admiration, are a gentile woman near Tyre, who changed the mind of Jesus on racism – the dogs under the table do eat the children's crumbs; also a scribe in Jerusalem who said that to love God and your neighbour was more than the temple sacrifices; a woman who put all her living, her two coins, into the collecting box in the temple; and another woman who anointed Jesus for burial whether she knew what she was doing or not. These are the only people who come out of the story well.

Even God is outmanoeuvred by the blindness and perversity of human beings. He speaks in Mark at the baptism and the transfiguration, 'You are my son', 'This is my son'. He also speaks through the person of the owner of the vineyard, and what he says there is 'They will respect my son' (12.6). But do they? Luke, copying this, saw the problem – how can omniscience be caught out? And he adds the word, 'perhaps': 'Perhaps they will respect my son.' It is the only place in the New Testament where this Greek word *isōs*, for 'perhaps', ever comes.

So, this is Mark's book. He calls it Good News, but nothing in the story suggests that it is good news. There are no appearances of Jesus after his burial. There is no mention of the Church. The twelve would have been incapable of running a whelk stall, let alone a church, as Mark describes them (contrast Matthew, who calls them 'blessed' – 'Blessed are your eyes for they see; blessed are you, Simon Barjonah'). There is no ascension into heaven as there is in Luke and Acts. There is no gift of the Spirit as there is in Acts and in John's Gospel. There is no account of the founding of churches as in Luke–Acts right the way across the Mediterranean to Rome. When we read Mark, what we are left with is simply the words of the young man in white who is not even called an angel, and we hear these words over the shoulders of the unbelieving and disobedient women, 'You will see him in the future', *opsesthe*. One of these women is described as the mother of James and Joses, and Mark had told us earlier on who James and Joses were – they were the brothers of Jesus. His mother was called Mary, and his brothers, James and Joses. So even Mary doesn't come out of it well. She is one of the unbelieving women, who go to anoint the body on the day of the resurrection and say nothing to anybody because they are afraid.

The future is all that we are left with. Jam tomorrow, no jam today. We are like Abraham who only got enough space in the promised land to bury his dead. As Mark sees it, it is all faith and hope, nothing to hang on to now. This is how Mark communicates the gospel to us. It is foolishness. It is for faith, because this is how God works. The foolishness of God and the foolishness of his gospel make fools of the readers. God puts us through a series of frictions, of trials, as we read the book, of humiliations. First of all we identify with the Twelve – surely they are our models. No, they are not. Then we identify with the women at the tomb. No, they are wrong too. Then we identify with Jesus perhaps, but his last words are, 'My God, my God, why hast thou forsaken me?' The darkness has entered into his soul and he thinks he has been a failure. We might say 'What about the tearing of the temple veil?' This is God's act, from top to bottom, so it was not from the bottom upwards, but from the top downwards. It could be interpreted in two ways – either as a sign of God's anger, that he was angry with Jesus, and that he was on the side of those who were crucifying him, or it could be that he was on the side of Jesus; we are not told how to interpret the tearing of the veil. Commentators have hung on to one thing at this point in the book – the centurion at the foot of the cross. And they have said, 'Well, at any rate he had faith because he said that certainly this man was God's son'; but is it faith? If you look at it in its context, Jesus has cried out 'My God, my God, why hast thou forsaken me?' and someone has said 'Let's give him a drink. He's calling for Elijah; let's give him a drink; see if Elijah will come to take him down.' They give him the drink, and Elijah doesn't come, and Jesus dies and then Mark says of the centurion, when he saw that he so died, 'That is it.' The experiment had produced a negative result. He said 'Certainly this fellow (*houtos ho anthrōpos*) was God's son', meaning that he wasn't. It is the final cynical remark of the whole book. It is ironical because it is true but it is not what the centurion intends. At any rate this is one way of understanding Mark's centurion.

So, as we read this book we are victims of God's decision to work through foolishness and make fools of his agents, make a laughing stock of us; we are mocked by everybody. God makes monkeys of us all, just as he did with Jonah. Jonah did not want to go to Nineveh but God forced him to it, into the fish and out of the fish and then on to Nineveh. And then God let him down; there was no destruction of Nineveh. God changed his mind. So Jonah was angry. God says to Jonah, 'Are you right to be angry?' and Jonah says, 'Yes, mortally angry.' This is how we feel when we get to the end of Mark. It has been a waste of time to read this silly book.

And this is also how it was with Jeremiah. He says, 'You have duped me, Lord, and I have been your dupe. You have outwitted me and prevailed. All the day long I have been made a laughing-stock. Everyone ridicules me.' This is how you feel when you have read Mark. And this is how other people have thought about Mark's book. You can see this from looking up the lists of how many copies have been made of it. The earliest copies were written on papyrus. On papyrus there are 19 bits of Matthew, 9 bits of Luke, 22 bits of John's Gospel, but there are only 3 bits of Mark. They did not bother to copy it. They did not like it. Moreover, they did not quote it very much. If you look at any index of quotations from the New Testament, at the back of any of the Christian writers of the earlier centuries, you will find that Mark is hardly ever quoted; Matthew and Luke are quoted instead. And you could get almost the whole of Mark out of Matthew and Luke, all except a very few small bits.

There was no patristic commentary written on Mark by people like Jerome, Augustine, Origen. The first commentary on Mark was written by an unknown Irish monk, between the years 600 and 650, and first published by Oxford University Press in 1998. He knew that he was the first person to write a commentary on Mark. Living in Ireland in the seventh century you were not off centre or in an obscure place; being on the coast you were a centre of travel and he knew enough to know that no one else had written a commentary on Mark before him.

This is what we feel when we read Mark, this unpopular Gospel, and we can see why it was unpopular. We don't feel like this with Matthew, Luke or with John. They all fell for the temptation to provide a happy ending to the book. Matthew: the presence of the risen Christ till the end of the age, and the mission to the gentiles; Luke and Acts: all one book, the ascension, Pentecost, the worldwide mission up as far as Rome; John: the faith of Thomas, ('my Lord and my God'), but in John's Gospel there has been no suffering, no shame, no darkness, no mocking of Jesus. When we read Mark, what we say is there is nothing we can do except wait, wait without anything to hang on to, without any evidence, it is just that the young man said it. We can compare this with a famous passage in the Old Testament, the end of Habakkuk: 'The fig tree has no buds, the vines bear no harvest, the olive crop fails, the orchards yield no food, the fold is bereft of its flock and there are no cattle in the stalls. Even so, I exult in the Lord and rejoice in the God who saves me.' You can imagine Mark rewriting that for his own time: 'The women said nothing to anybody. The Jerusalem church still keeps the Mosaic law, the Pauline churches are divided, Peter and Paul are dead. Nero was not impressed. There were four emperors in one year and still Antichrist has not come, nor has Christ. Most of his contemporaries have died. Even so, I shall go on waiting. I shall stay awake until the sun is darkened and the moon does not give her light.'

Mark's Gospel has one, and only one, long speech of Jesus. It is chapter 13, the Marcan apocalypse, the signs before Christ comes, the history of the world seen from the crucifixion, seen looking forward. And the point is, things get worse and worse; they get worse and then Antichrist comes; they get worse still before Christ comes. That is the prospect of the people for whom Mark wrote.

Another way to think of Mark's Gospel is to think of it as a joke. Good News in the form of bad news, that's a sort of joke already. And with jokes you mustn't ask for more. I am supplied with jokes by medical students, which are not really repeatable, but here's one that is repeatable, and nothing to do with medicine. Two men in the desert see a caravan and they want refreshment, and they crawl up to it and they say, 'Give us water,' and they say, 'We've only got sponge cake.' They see another caravan and they say, 'Give us water,' and they say, 'We've only got custard.' They see another caravan and they crawl up to it and say, 'Give us water,' and they say, 'We've only got whipped cream.' One man says to the other, 'Odd, wasn't it?' and the other one says, 'I confess I did think it a trifle bizarre.' If you were then to say to me, 'Did they get the water?' I'd know you hadn't seen the joke.

The oldest joke in the Bible, possibly the oldest joke in the world, is the birth of Isaac. Geriatric sex. Perhaps you know the riddle: What does SAGA stand for? Sex Again Granny, it's August. Well, Abraham laughs when he is told that Sarah is going to have a baby (Genesis 17.17). Sarah laughs (Genesis 18.12). God says 'Call him Isaac', because Isaac means he laughs (Genesis 17.19). Abraham was nearly 100 and Sarah was in her 90s and they had been trying for years. And Paul says this is what faith is. Doing what Abraham did. Ignoring the death of his body, as good as dead. Taking no account of the deadness of Sarah's womb, hoping against hope, he tried again and again and one time it worked, and everyone laughed. Mark's story-line ends in hopelessness. This is where faith begins. Was there any point in going on? No, no point. That is the reason for going on in hope against hope. We know that Mark had meditated on the story of the sacrifice of Isaac in Genesis 22, a story that used to terrify us as children. Might my father do the same thing to me? In Genesis 22, three times God says, or an angel says, 'Your son, your one and only son' (verses 2, 12 and 16), 'you're to sacrifice him'. In Mark, also three times, Jesus is called 'My one and only son', *huios agapētos, ho huios mou ho agapētos.* 'You are my one and only son' (1.11). At the transfiguration, 'This is my one and only son' (9.7). And in the parable of the vineyard he had one left to send, his one and only son. There is another echo of Genesis 22 in Mark when Jesus says, 'Sit here while I pray.' This is the same as in Genesis 22.5, 'Stay here with the donkey while I and the boy go ahead.' And Matthew, at the parallel point copying Mark, has made the parallel with Genesis 22 more exact by changing one word: instead of *hōde* he has *autou*, an unusual use of the genitive to describe place.

The really terrifying verse in the Genesis story is when Isaac says to Abraham, 'Father, here are the fire and the wood, but where is the sheep for a sacrifice?' (Genesis 22.7). And there is the terrible ambiguous and uncommunicative answer of Abraham, 'God will provide himself with a sheep for a sacrifice, my son.' We are left to wonder to ourselves, at what point did Isaac realize what was going to happen? He must have got there by the time he was bound and laid on the altar on top of the wood. According to Genesis he seldom spoke again. Only when he was old and blind, a pathetic old man longing for a dish of chilli con carne, wanting to bless Esau, his older son, against God's will, tricked by Jacob and Rebecca into blessing him instead, and then he speaks, sending Jacob away to get a wife in Paddan Aram. Isaac had been traumatized by the event on the mountain. Remember how he needed the wife Rebecca to comfort him after his mother Sarah had died. He is pathetic.

In Mark's account, Jesus takes the place of Isaac. Jesus realizes this finally and most clearly in Gethsemane, where he says, 'Father, Abba Father'. And like Isaac he seldom speaks after this. On Good Friday in Mark's Gospel, Jesus only speaks twice, once to Pilate saying 'It's you who says so', *su legeis*; once to God when he says 'Why have you forsaken me?' Though they taunt him to prophesy he keeps silence and Pilate is amazed. Jesus is the new Isaac. Paul had seen it too in writing to the Romans, 'God did not spare his own son', compare Genesis 22.16, 'because you did not spare your son'. So Jesus is the sheep that God has provided for sacrifice in Mark; but not only Jesus; his followers are to be sacrificed also. 'Take up your cross and follow me' (Mark 8.34). 'Drink the cup that I drink, share in my baptism' (Mark 10). Mark answers Isaac's question, 'Where is the sacrifice?' It is Jesus. And it is you, my dear reader.

Mark has deliberately arranged his book in order to make fools of us. The distribution of the miracle stories in Mark shows this. Mark has 18 detailed miracles performed by Jesus – the highest rate of miracles per page in all four Gospels. And 15 of these 18 come in the first half of the book. Mark leads us to expect a miracle of salvation, 'I shall not die but live', like the healing of the sick, like peace to people who are disintegrated, like food to the hungry, the end of the storm, life to the dead. That is how we feel in the first half of Mark's book, but when we get to the second half, we are told straight off, 'The son of man must suffer, and anyone who wants to be a follower must also suffer.' 'Everyone will be salted with fire' (Mark 9.49), a saying of Jesus in Mark that is not copied by Matthew and Luke. It is a parody of a saying in Leviticus 2.13, 'Every sacrifice will be salted with salt.' But now it is not sacrifices that have to be salted, but everybody. You are the sacrifice, and you are not to be salted with salt; you are to be salted with fire, that is, to be destroyed. Everyone will be made acceptable to God by destruction. This is Mark's main theme, this is the point of his book, to get people ready for destruction. And maybe he knew about Nero, how he made

Roman candles out of the Christians, tying them to stakes in his garden and lighting them to illuminate his evening parties.

Peter and the rest of the Twelve never get this point in Mark. The woman with the two coins got it, because she put in her whole *bios*, her whole livelihood, and the woman who anoints his body for burial. Mark has only two healing miracle stories in the second half of his book: one is the boy who is deaf and dumb in chapter 9, 'He became as one dead,' so that the majority said 'He's died.' Jesus came and raised him and he arose. Death and resurrection, each one said twice for emphasis. That is the only way into life – death and resurrection – no miracles to save us from that.

Bartimaeus in chapter 10 is the next miracle that comes after the middle of the book, and when he receives his sight, he followed him in the way, *hodō*; 'I am the way', 'Christianity – the way', he followed him in the way to Jerusalem to death and resurrection. The third miracle is the cursing of the fig tree, the only negative miracle in the book. Totally destructive. The only miracle that is done in Jerusalem by Jesus. He is mocked during the crucifixion for not doing miracles. 'He saved others – he cannot save himself.' He can only cure others by not saving himself, by death and resurrection, and they must follow him, drinking the same cup, being baptized with the same baptism. Mark rubs our noses in humiliation. Joseph of Arimathaea asks for the body of Jesus, *sōma*, Pilate donates the corpse, *ptōma*, a word that Matthew and Luke avoid here. It comes from a verb meaning to fall, collapse, *piptō*, and it refers to a corpse that is very dead. Where the corpse is there the vultures will be gathered. It is used in Mark also of the headless body of John the Baptist. Matthew and Luke and John avoid using this word of Jesus but Mark knows that the gospel is an offence. This is why the women are afraid and silent. They had gone to the tomb expecting to find the dead body and to do the necessary, as it were to draw a line under the whole incident and go back to Galilee to hot suppers cooked by Peter's mother-in-law, and fishing and life as it used to be before Jesus had come. And then, if the young man is right, if God is actually on the side of Jesus and if this is what God does to his son, then say nothing to anybody.

So Mark leaves us with nothing. No theology, no christology, no ethics, no eschatology, no ministry and sacraments, no church history. Thank goodness. These are all things that divide us from one another. And Mark keeps them away. He just gives us a story, a story of disaster. Out of that we might have faith. That is what the book assumes, that you might read it in a different way, with faith in a God who can do anything, even raise the dead, and that you might have love for him and for others and hope that all will be well in the end when the Kingdom comes.

Mark's Gospel is, I believe, the best of the Gospels for the twenty-first century; it was rediscovered in the nineteenth century underneath Matthew, Luke and John, thanks to Karl Lachmann. It was explained to us in the twentieth century, thanks to William Wrede, James Hardy Ropes and Robert Henry Lightfoot and literary critics who came in to show us how to read a book, a thing that Christians had forgotten.

It is the best book for the twenty-first century because it is so utterly subversive. Western European culture will need some subversive people to do something about its capitalism and its love of self. The one character who is the model in Mark's Gospel is the child and the child is there as representative of people who are unskilled, nobodies; who have no status. The child appears twice, in chapter 9 and in chapter 10, and in both cases, Jesus hugs them. They are the only people that he does hug. The rich will find it hard to enter the kingdom of God. The first will be last and the last will be first. Life will be through death; death is the only way forward. This will be necessary for the twenty-first century, when what we will all be trying to do is to live as long as possible and be as rich as possible. But notice one thing about this rich man: he wants to know what he should do. He has kept the commandments and Jesus says he lacks one thing – 'Sell what you have and give to the poor', and the man goes away sad. And it says there in Mark, 'Jesus looked at him and loved him.' It is the only instance of Jesus loving somebody. He loves the person who can't do it. This again is subversive and this is what is so good about Mark. He saw that his readers would never be able to accept his book, and he was right. Matthew and Luke were trying to suppress it by taking most of it and putting it forward in a different way. The people who wrote the longer and shorter additions in chapter 16 were also trying to give it a happy ending; but now at last we see Mark's book again and people have brought it to our attention so that we can read it as it really was. We see the impossibility of the demand, 'Destroy your life! That's the only way to preserve it.' And we know we can't do it, but the man who couldn't do it was the one that Jesus loved. Away success! Welcome failure! That is the good news.

6

The Passion Narrative in Mark's Gospel

MARK WROTE AS AN EVANGELIST, not as a historian. Neither in the passion narrative, nor in the book as a whole, did he give a historical answer to the question, Why was Jesus executed? He provided very little insight into the motives of the chief priests as they sought to kill Jesus; he did not make it clear what Pilate's views were, or what role he played in the case; he did not explain the mental processes of Judas Iscariot that led him to make an arrangement with the authorities. The historical question – in the sense in which we understand history, that is human motives and intentions and purposes as they lead up to the making of decisions – was not dealt with by Mark. We can see that this is so from the diversity of answers that have been given to the historical question over the last two hundred years, many of them claiming to be based on Mark's account. The reason why Mark did not do what we might have expected him to do may be in part because he lacked the information, but it is more likely that this kind of writing was not what he was aiming at. He wanted to write a Gospel and he wanted to preach the good news of God to the reader of his book. What he was interested in, therefore, was the divine aspect of the events that he included, both in the book as a whole and in the passion narrative in particular. These things had to happen: the Son of Man had come with the one purpose of giving his life as a ransom for many; he died to fulfil the Scriptures and establish the covenant. The death and resurrection of Jesus, as Mark understood them, were God's will. If Mark can persuade his readers of that, then they will not be interested in the human decisions through which the divine will was accomplished. To the believer, it will not matter what the purpose of the sanhedrin was, or of Pilate, or of Judas: the believer will be interested solely in the purpose of God, and this is what Mark claims to know, and to be able to convey to his reader through his book.

The evangelist must be approached as a preacher. It is tautologous to say so. Throughout the book, but especially when he tells the story of the passion, he is proclaiming the good news of God. To hear what Mark is saying, the reader must enter into that attitude of mind that is appropriate to receiving the gospel, what Paul calls the hearing of faith. This will include close attention to what is being said, openness to new and offensive ideas, a willingness to change and to be changed, and a readiness to obey.

By the passion narrative is meant the whole story from the reference to the approach of Passover at the beginning of chapter 14, to the flight and silence of the women in chapter 16. The last sentence of the Gospel is: 'And they said nothing to anyone, because they were afraid.' This is where Mark's Gospel ends in *Codex Sinaiticus* and *Codex Vaticanus* and in one much later Greek manuscript. This is also where it ends according to some of the early Christian writers, and in some of the most ancient translations from Greek into other languages. It seems to have been the place at which the even earlier copies of Mark that were used by Matthew and Luke had ended. Many writers of the twentieth century thought that it was Mark's intention to stop here and, however surprising this may seem to us, it cannot be denied that it would have been very difficult to have followed the sentence about the silence of the women with a further paragraph continuing the story without contradicting what had just been said. For if the disciples must go to Galilee to see Jesus, and if it was necessary to tell them to go, as Mark implies, and if the women did not do this, how could the story proceed? This ending clearly did not please Matthew and Luke, who each adjusted the Marcan text in his own way in order to allow the narrative to run on, nor did it please the early editors who added various endings. Mark, as it stands, could not have been continued without a major hiatus at this point. The best solution is therefore to think that this is where Mark intended to finish his book.

The importance of this is that, in this Gospel, the resurrection of Jesus, though of course it is firmly believed in, and is referred to on at least eight distinct occasions in the second half of the book, is not presented as a separate event, to be detached from the narrative of the passion. The reader does not see Jesus again, after his burial, on the page of the book; he only overhears the young man (not even an angel) say that he is risen, and is invited to see the space where he was laid, but is no longer. The resurrection provides the way in which the passion narrative is to be read – it is how faith receives the story of the death of Jesus. God has approved of Jesus: he has declared him his Son, the Beloved, and he has commanded the disciples to attend to him. They are now to live for his coming as the judge of the world, and this means that they are to put his teaching into practice by following him, to destruction. Here we have an explanation of the terror of the women with which the book ends. If this young man is right, if God has endorsed the teaching of Jesus by raising him from the dead, then what Jesus said is true, and will apply to everybody: we must all disown ourselves, take up the instruments of our execution, follow Jesus and lose our lives. Anyone who tries to save himself will be lost. And if this is how God deals with his beloved Son, how will he deal with those who are the Son's brothers and sisters and mother? The reaction of the women is the only reaction that is possible, apart from faith.

Of the four passion narratives in the New Testament, Mark's is probably the earliest, and the other three can best be seen as attempts to retell the same story, with the intention of improving on what Mark had done. It is a question we need not decide, whether the later passion narratives are, in fact, improvements on the earliest, or whether they reveal a decline from a previous and better way of telling the story. On the other hand, it is of the greatest importance to recognize that Mark's account must not be read with those of Matthew, Luke or John in mind: readers of Mark must free themselves from any influence the other Gospels may have had upon them. For example, Matthew's account of the centurion and his men confessing faith in Jesus as Son of God must not be allowed to prejudice the reader into thinking that the centurion in Mark is necessarily making a statement of faith. Here it is more likely that the centurion, along with all the other characters involved in the crucifixion, speaks the truth without meaning to do so. It is intended as the final, bitter, cynical remark – the irony is that it is true. In Matthew, there is no ambiguity, for divine intervention in the form of earthquakes and resurrections has destroyed ambiguity. In Mark, on the other hand, the story can be read in either of two ways: as failure or as success. Similarly, Luke's portrayal of Jesus as the one who dies in faith, praying for forgiveness for his executioners, assuring his penitent companion of salvation, and entrusting his spirit into the hands of his Father, must not prevent the reader of Mark from seeing Jesus in this Gospel as the one whose faith is destroyed by events. In the same way, the faith of the mother of Jesus and of the disciple whom Jesus loved, in John, must not obscure the isolation of Jesus in Mark. Here it is said of the disciples that they all forsook him and fled, one of them even preferring the shame of nakedness to being associated with Jesus, and his mother (if that is who is meant by Mary the mother of James the younger and Joseph) looks on from a distance and disobeys the young man's command, because she is afraid.

Everything, therefore, that is known from other sources must be subtracted from the memory, if Mark's account is to be heard and understood and received. And when this is done, then it becomes clear why other accounts of the passion were later thought to be needed, and were supplied by Matthew, Luke and John. Mark's passion was too drastic and too terrifying; it was a prescription for martyrdom; and it offered comfort only to those who were willing to forgo comfort.

Long before the passion narrative began, Mark had prepared his readers for the death of Jesus. As early as the first group of conflict stories in chapters 2 and 3, it had been foretold that the days would come when the bridegroom would be taken away from his friends; and it was at the end of that section that Mark recorded the first movement of the opponents of Jesus to destroy him. But the explicit and repeated predictions of the passion and resurrection begin immediately after Peter's confession of faith that Jesus is the Christ. It is as if Mark were saying, There can be no faith in Christ that is not faith in Christ crucified. In a sense, therefore, readers have been prepared for the final events long before they read about them. And yet, they have not. Nothing that was said in the earlier part of the book could have led them to expect that Jesus would pray that the cup should be taken away from him; that is, that God would change what was already destined to happen, and had already been foretold by Jesus himself. And nothing that was said before the passion narrative began could have prepared the way for the last words of Jesus in Mark's Gospel, the exit-line of the book's central character: 'My God, my God, why have you forsaken me?' The events of the last day, when they finally take place, overwhelm even Jesus himself, and they put the readers' faith to the most severe test. Destruction is total and unlimited, both for Jesus and for his followers. The good news is presented as a stumbling-block.

But even so, if readers go back to the earlier sections of the book, they will find that there have been hints and clues that they may have missed at the first reading, which they can now see in a new light. (It is a necessary presupposition that Mark meant his book to be read more than once.) For example, Jesus had said that everybody would be salted with fire and his words contained an echo of a passage in Leviticus: 'Salt shall accompany all offerings.' A scribe of Mark's Gospel, copying it out, added these words from Leviticus to the text of the Gospel, to explain the meaning of the saying of Jesus. What salt had been to the sacrifices under the Law, fire (and therefore destruction) will be in the new order that Jesus has inaugurated. Nothing, Mark believed, could survive the tribulation and God's final judgement and entry into the kingdom of God without passing through the process of total disintegration. The stones and buildings of the temple were to be thrown down, the sun would be darkened, the moon extinguished, and the stars would fall from the sky. There would be a total black-out, and only after this would the Son of Man come to gather the elect. Nothing would be exempt from this rule, not even the Son of Man himself who said it, least of all the Son of Man. By the time he dies, all his confidence and faith have been destroyed.

Mark's way of bringing his readers to understand the destruction of Jesus' faith is subtle, and it is important to see how he achieves it. The emphasis is not placed on the physical suffering of Jesus, but on the mental. The passion is described as brainwashing, which reduces Jesus to total disintegration, not by the pain of crucifixion itself, nor by the preliminary scourging, which are only mentioned briefly, but by what is said to him. He is destroyed by words. His death is by mocking.

Mark realizes that the most painful and effective form of mocking is when one is ridiculed for what one is, and not for what one is not. The most powerful weapon of the torturer is the truth, for it is the words of our friends which hurt us most, because they have access to the truth about us. If it is the case that the truth will make you free, it is also the case that it may destroy you first. All the opponents of Jesus in Mark speak the truth and, in Greek, the questions put to him can be read as statements: the chief priest says, 'You are the Christ, the Son of the Blessed'; Pilate greets him with, 'You are the king of the Jews', and continues to refer to him by this title, which Mark reserves for the account of the passion; the soldiers dress Jesus in the emperor's purple and put an imperial crown on his head and hail him as Caesar; the passers-by congratulate him as the one who destroys the temple and rebuilds it in three days; the chief priests say that he saved others but cannot save himself; and finally, when he is dead, the centurion declares him to be the Son of God. It is all true, and the readers know that Jesus knows it too. He had been addressed as God's Son at the baptism, he was the Beloved on whom God's favour rested. But how can he be this, when these things are happening to him? When Jesus cries out, 'Eloi, Eloi', some of the people present maliciously misinterpret Eloi as Elias, and say, 'He is calling for Elijah'. Then one of them sets up the final experiment: he gives Jesus the vinegar to preserve him for long enough to allow Elijah time to come from heaven and take Jesus down from the cross. It was, in a way, fair enough, because had not Elijah himself submitted God to a similar experiment on Mount Carmel? But Jesus dies without any supernatural intervention, and when the centurion sees that the result of the test is negative, he dismisses Jesus as a charlatan: 'This fellow really was the Son of God!'

Jesus has been destroyed by the contradiction between who he believes himself to be, and what is happening to him. He is God's Son, yet he is being put to death. The contradiction is driven into him by the mocking of his opponents. And the readers' faith too is being tested: can they believe in a God who does not save by miracles, and provides no proof that the good news is true?

The darkness over the whole earth, and the tearing of the temple veil, are not signs that demonstrate the truth of Jesus indisputably. They are ambiguous; they declare God's wrath, but leave open the question, With whom is God angry? With Jesus, or with those who are crucifying him? To Jesus, it seems that God has forsaken him. The darkness has entered his own soul. And this is the understanding of the other characters in the story. Only the evangelist has a different view, and this is what he wants to communicate to his readers.

The final speech of Jesus before the passion narrative began was made in private, on the Mount of Olives, to the four disciples whom Jesus had called first, at the very beginning of the book. This speech foretells the passion of the followers of Jesus, and it is thus an introduction to the passion of Jesus, since he and his followers must go by the same route. So, through reading the prediction of what will happen to them, the readers can foresee what will happen to Jesus. For example, Jesus has warned them against those who perform signs and wonders; they are false Christs and false prophets. With this in mind, they will not expect Jesus to save himself by a miracle, or God to intervene on his behalf.

But they will believe that God will raise up Jesus from the dead, because they have heard in this speech that the Son of Man is to come with great power and glory at the end of the age, to gather the elect. Just as the disciples are to go through destruction to salvation, and just as the universe is to be destroyed and remade, so the Son of Man must suffer, die and be raised up. The law that everyone is to be salted with the fire that destroys applies universally.

Now in this final speech of Jesus, the disciples are instructed not to be anxious in advance about what they will say when they are brought into court to be tried; they are to say whatever is given to them at that hour. Then Jesus adds, 'Because it is not you who speak, but the Holy Spirit.' This might have led readers to expect that Jesus would make a final speech to his opponents, inspired by the Spirit, either before the Jewish sanhedrin or in Pilate's court. But he says little in the former, and in the latter his silence is such that Pilate is amazed – and so are the readers. (Mark draws attention to incidents through the characters in the narrative. He will use Pilate again in the same way, when it comes to emphasizing the speed with which Jesus has died.) As Mark presents the passion, God has given Jesus nothing to say: the Holy Spirit has not spoken through him and in this respect it is true, as Jesus says, that God has forsaken him.

But it should be noticed that in Mark it was not, in fact, said that the Holy Spirit would speak through the disciples. (It is different in Matthew.) In Mark, it was only said that the Spirit would speak, not the disciples, and it was left unclear in whom the Spirit would operate. When Jesus is brought into court, he says to Pilate, 'You speak'; and Pilate, the chief priest and all the others say who Jesus is, and what he does.

The Spirit speaks through the opponents of Jesus, and through them declares him God's Son, the Christ, the king of the Jews, the Saviour who cannot save himself. The inspiration of God works through the human, unbelieving, malicious intention to mock. God is not fastidious over the methods he uses to achieve his purposes. Just as he is no respecter of persons, so he is also totally without scruples about the means he will use to reach his ends.

The disciples are conspicuously absent from the passion narrative as it moves towards its climax. Jesus first predicts that Judas will hand him over, then that they will all be offended, and finally that Peter will disown him three times. The fulfilment of these predictions happens in the order in which they were made: Judas, the ten, and finally Peter. Moreover, all this is how it must be: the scattering of the flock had been foretold in Scripture, and was part of God's plan. Jesus had to suffer alone: the scene in Gethsemane demonstrated it also and made it clear to Jesus, and to the disciples, and to the readers, how it must be. The form of the story implies the revelation of a truth because there had been instances before in Mark in which three or four disciples were taken apart, and in each case something was disclosed – the resurrection of a dead person, the future glory of the Son of Man, the suffering of the disciples before the end. What is revealed in Gethsemane is that Jesus must be unaccompanied as he goes to do God's will and the three disciples cannot even stay awake and pray.

The two paragraphs that speak of the failure of the disciples, first of Judas, then of the rest, stand one on either side of a passage to which the editors of a recent Greek Testament have given the title, 'The Institution of the Lord's Supper'. The Marcan narrative, however, contains nothing that warrants such a description. There is no command to do anything in the future, for this was a single and unique occasion, not the institution of a rite that was to be repeated.

The passage must be read as it stands. Jesus gives them bread and commands them to take it, declaring that it is his body; he gives them a cup from which they all drink, and only then does he say that it is his blood. They enact their destruction of him, body and blood, by eating and drinking bread and wine. They are made to take on responsibility for his coming death. When Mark surrounds one story with two parts of another, it is always to throw light on the central story. So here the surrounding paragraphs that predict failure interpret the meaning of the eating and drinking: the disciples will be like those people in the Psalms who eat God's people like bread, they are the enemies and foes who eat up the flesh. The same language of biting, devouring and consuming was still being used by Paul when he wrote to the Galatians. And there was the memorable story of David refusing to drink the water from the well at Bethlehem for which his companions had risked their lives because he said that it would have been to have drunk their blood. But Jesus makes his disciples drink, and thus be responsible for his death, and then he tells them what they have done. To be responsible for the death of Jesus is the obverse of the belief that Christ died for our sins: the disciples are the cause of his death, and liable for it. Jesus relates himself to them as food to him who eats it: just as the eater lives by the destruction of his food, so the disciples live by the death of Jesus.

The disciples must therefore be absent from the narrative, because Jesus dies for them. Their absence is part of the good news because it makes it clear that what is being done is being done by Jesus, alone, and it is being well done. He can only save others by not saving himself. He must go forward alone and be the single, isolated sufferer who stands in for all the rest. The name Barabbas means son of the father, and this is what everyone is – Jesus dies in order that Barabbas, Everyman, may be freed.

The story of the passion is therefore told by Mark in a way that is rich in allusion to the Scriptures in order to explain and draw attention to Jesus' obedience to God's will at the point where everyone else fails, and to show that his obedience cancels and redeems their disobedience. Jesus goes on beyond what anyone else can do or suffer, to be the unique and final agent of God, allowing himself to be broken and destroyed totally. God's gift is both a present and an invitation: the present is that Christ died for us, the invitation is to suffer with him. Mark makes it clear that the present must be received first, before it is possible to answer the invitation. Jesus must drink the cup before the disciples can drink also.

Mark's book began with Jesus proclaiming the nearness of the kingdom of God and performing miracles, and the miracles led Peter to say that Jesus was the Christ. But a Christ who only does miracles is not the Christ of Mark's faith and it is immediately apparent that Peter is still the spokesman of Satan. Mark believes in a Christ who must die and Mark also believes that discipleship is following Jesus to destruction. That is the way into the kingdom of God.

The expression, 'The kingdom of God', comes twice in the passion narrative. First, Jesus declares at the supper that he will not drink wine again until he drinks it new in the kingdom of God. He is looking beyond the coming destruction of this creation to the new age when God will rule the world and the elect will be gathered together for eternal life. The other instance is the last in Mark's Gospel, and it is unlike all the other thirteen references in that it is not within a saying of Jesus, but is part of the evangelist's own comment. Joseph of Arimathea, he says, was himself also looking forward to the kingdom of God. Joseph, then, is like Jesus: both are living in hope for the time when God will be king. Jesus has been taken away but one day he will return as the Son of Man, and his followers will see him. Meanwhile, Joseph asks for the body of Jesus, and Pilate graciously grants him the corpse. Mark changes the words: he asked for the *sōma* and he was given the *ptōma*, a word that comes from a verb meaning to fall, or collapse. Joseph is the symbol of all believers for he is the man with the corpse, the dead, ruined remains of Jesus which, Mark believes, is both God's present to the world, its ransom and reconciliation with God and God's invitation to submit to destruction as the only way into life.

Though nothing is known for certain about the place

where this Gospel was written, or about the time of its writing, or about its author, it would be consistent with the point of view that the book expressed to think that the author and his intended readers believed themselves to be threatened with imminent extinction. Mark (whoever he was) met the needs of the time by composing a narrative that required readers to respond with a faith that dispensed with reassurance in the present and trusted in a God who would act beyond this world. He believed in and wrote a book of good news about the God with whom all things are possible.

7

The Ending of Mark's Gospel

PROFESSOR C. F. EVANS said to me once that a good way to teach Mark's Gospel was to begin with the end of the book, at 16.8. When it can be demonstrated that the evangelist does not tell his readers what happened next, but leaves them to make up their own minds whether they will believe what the young man has said, or not, it will then be easier to show what sort of book we are dealing with when we read Mark: a Gospel (whatever that is), not a collection of an apostle's reminiscences.

In point of fact, it was the question of the ending of Mark's Gospel that, historically speaking, opened up new ways of reading it. When R. H. Lightfoot[1] was arguing that the evangelist meant to stop at 16.8, and that there never had been a lost ending or any intention of continuing the narrative further, the first objection that was always raised was: Surely he must have meant to include at least one account of an appearance of Jesus after the resurrection; this was the most important event in the life of Peter; Mark could not have missed it out.[2] And the answer that was given was: Mark is not that sort of a book; you are reading it with inappropriate expectations; you are repeating the mistake of the person who is told a joke and then asks, 'What happened next?' What used to be called 'The Marcan Hypothesis', the theory that in Mark's 'presentation of the life of Christ the facts of history are set down with a minimum of disarrangement, interpretation, and embellishment',[3] fell to pieces as a result of the study of the ending of the Gospel: if it were that kind of book, it would not end in this way; since it did end at 16.8, it cannot be that kind of book.

But is there any need to take up the question of the ending of Mark again, after so much has been written on the subject in the last fifty years? That the Gospel is complete cannot be regarded as one of the generally accepted results of biblical criticism. Three examples must suffice, arranged in chronological order.

First, in 1971 the United Bible Societies published *A Textual Commentary on the Greek New Testament*, subtitled 'A Companion Volume to the United Bible Societies' Greek New Testament (third edition)', by Bruce M. Metzger 'on behalf of and in cooperation with the Editorial Committee of the United Bible Societies' Greek New Testament': Kurt Aland, Matthew Black, Carlo M. Martini, Bruce M. Metzger and Allen Wikgren. The two volumes, the *Greek New Testament* and the *Textual Commentary*, are published in the same material and in the same colour, and the unwary reader might think the second had the same authority as the first. After discussing the textual evidence for the various endings of Mark, Metzger and his colleagues continue in a footnote:

> Three possibilities are open: (a) the evangelist intended to close his Gospel at this place; or (b) the Gospel was never finished; or, as seems most probable, (c) the Gospel accidentally lost its last leaf before it was multiplied by transcription.[4]

One might dismiss this reference to the hypothesis of a lost ending of Mark as a suggestion made in a footnote twenty years ago; but as recently as 1992 it was still being said of Mark's Gospel that it is 'quite possibly truncated at both ends'.[5]

Second, in 1989 the University Presses of Oxford and Cambridge published The Revised English Bible. After their translation of Mark 16.1–8, as if it were another paragraph but still part of verse 8, they printed what is known as the Shorter Ending, without any sign in the text to indicate that this was not in all manuscripts, etc. After a double space, there follows their translation of the Longer Ending, verses 9–20; and there are notes at the foot of the page that explain the problem. Anyone asked to read Mark 16.1–8, who had not studied the footnotes, would assume that the passage ended immediately before the beginning of verse 9, and would therefore include the Shorter Ending in the reading. Was this, however, simply a printer's error that escaped the eye of the proof reader? There was a reprint of the book in the year of publication, but there was no correction of the text at this point.

Third, a major commentary on Mark was published in 1993, by Robert H. Gundry;[6] his view is that Mark 16.8 is not the last verse of the paragraph that began at 16.1, but the first verse of another paragraph that is incomplete. In this now mutilated paragraph the evangelist described how the disciples saw Jesus in Galilee in fulfilment of the prediction in Mark 14.28. Gundry provides twelve reasons for thinking that this is how Mark's Gospel originally ended, together with further notes. He does not, however, explain how the disciples received the message to go to Galilee, which 16.7 implies they needed; or provide a satisfactory account of why Mark has told his readers about the visit of the women to the tomb, if it was to have no connection with the continuation of the narrative of the disciples.

The suggestion that Mark intended to end his Gospel at 16.8 was first made by Wellhausen in 1903, and in taking up the topic again, over ninety years later, I want to draw attention to an English writer, the first English writer, I suppose, to support Wellhausen on this matter.[7] J. M. Creed's article, 'The Conclusion of the Gospel according to Saint Mark', was published in 1930,[8] eight years before R. H. Lightfoot's *Locality and Doctrine in the Gospels*, and as it has never been republished and is only available to those who have access to back numbers of the *Journal of Theological Studies*, I shall attempt to give a selective summary of the argument; but the reader should be warned that this is only a summary, and that the argument in the article is concise and, in some parts, obscure.

Creed begins by stating the problem of the variant readings: (i) the ending at 16.8 in אB, the old Syriac, codex *a*;[9] (ii) the Shorter Ending, in codex *k*; (iii) the last twelve verses of the received text. Neither (ii) nor (iii) is thought to be by Mark, but to end at 16.8 as in (i) would be very abrupt; hence 'many scholars are inclined to conjecture that a further paragraph recounting at the least the appearance of the risen Jesus to the disciples in Galilee, which the angel predicts in v. 7, has disappeared'. (Throughout the article, Creed refers to the young man in Mark 16.5–7 as an angel, though Mark himself does not describe him in this way.) Creed's intention, he says, is to argue that 'it is very improbable that the genuine Gospel was ever longer than it now is'; he refers to Wellhausen and E. Meyer, who both held the same view as Creed, but he believes that he is stating the argument in a different way from them.

He then notices briefly the hypotheses that have been framed to account for the supposed incompleteness of the Gospel, namely: (i) that the author died before finishing it; (ii) that the text was deliberately mutilated; and (iii) that it was mutilated by accident, and he finds them all inadequate as explanations of the conjecture that the text is incomplete, 'unless we are compelled to do so by the document itself'. This is the main purpose of the article, and what makes it so significant: Creed is attending to Mark's text, and enquiring whether there is anything in it that suggests incompleteness.

He then draws our attention to what he calls 'a strange incoherence' in the Marcan text; namely, the contradiction between what the women are commanded to do, in verse 7, and what they fail to do, in verse 8: they are charged to tell the disciples, but they remain silent. He says that this is 'a very startling phenomenon', which is not always remarked.

There is incoherence in the Marcan narrative – significant incoherence – but it is latent. So long as we stop at v. 8 it does not really matter. But, on the theory of the lost conclusion, how are we to proceed? The latent incoherence will at once become intolerable. For we must suppose one of two things: either the lost conclusion was continuous with the story of the women, or else it made a fresh start with the disciples and their vision of the Lord in Galilee. It is hard to combine either supposition with verses 7 and 8 of chapter xvi. For v. 8 has effectively dismissed the women from further immediate participation in events, while v. 7 urgently demands their intervention.

He then considers the suggestion that had been made a few years earlier by C. H. Turner, that the lost ending related how Jesus appeared to the women and quieted their fears, so that they were able to tell the disciples; but he criticizes this, on the ground that 'they said nothing to anybody' must mean 'they did not deliver the message'. 'If the narrative of the women at the tomb is to be linked up with narratives of the appearances, it is essential that the women should deliver the message.' Creed then draws our attention to the way in which Matthew and Luke have achieved this result: 'by suppressing the tell-tale words, "they said nothing to anybody"'; that was the only way in which they could make the story of the women lead on to the story of the disciples.

He then takes up the alternative hypothesis, that Mark made a fresh start with the journey of the disciples to Galilee, and refers to Kirsopp Lake's suggestion that the disciples had already left Jerusalem; that was why the women were unable to tell them what the 'angel' had said. But Creed points out that there is a decisive objection to this: 'The angel, on this theory, gives a message to the women which it was impossible for them to deliver. This ought not to be, and we may securely assume that it was not so.'

Creed then explains that what he is doing is asking how Mark could have proceeded, if he did; he must, Creed says, either have left 'the angel's message hanging in the air', or else he must have explained why it was not delivered to the disciples. Neither of these two courses seems probable. 'Internal evidence, therefore, as well as external probability, seems to point to the conclusion that the Marcan narrative never went beyond the words, "for they were afraid".'

Creed makes one further point: he suggests an explanation of how it was that the 'incoherence' arose. Mark, he thinks, was working on traditions that were already in existence; one of them was the story of the women at the tomb, which might

have 'but recently come into circulation'. He follows E.
Meyer in thinking that Mark inserted verse 7 into this traditional unit, without noticing that the silence of the women
would make it impossible for the narrative to continue – but,
in any case, he had no intention of continuing. The problem
only arose when Matthew and Luke wanted to link the story
of the women at the tomb to the account of appearances to
disciples. 'The absence of that link in Mark is an indication
that in his Gospel no narrative followed.'

The strength of Creed's argument that 16.8 was the
intended conclusion to the Gospel lies in the method that he
used: he paid attention to what Mark actually wrote; and he
asks, Having written this, in these words, could he have
written more? Creed challenges anyone who upholds the
hypothesis of a lost ending to the Gospel to say how that
ending could have followed on from verses 1–8, without
hiatus, contradiction or redundancy. He observes the distinction, which is not always made, between what happened (to
the women and the disciples, on Easter day) and what Mark
wrote (when he composed his book); it is a method of
studying a Gospel that has yielded rich results, but in 1930 it
was novel, and Creed should be honoured as one of the
earliest writers in England to approach a problem in the
Gospels in this way.

I do not intend to go further and offer an explanation as to
why Mark ended his Gospel thus. There has been no shortage
of interpretations. Was it that the evangelist had an anti-
Jerusalem bias – the apostles themselves ('his disciples and
Peter') never received the message from the young man,
therefore they did not believe in the resurrection, but were
still in sin? Or was it that the evangelist was engaged in a controversy between followers of Paul and the sort of people he
described as super-apostles (2 Corinthians 12.11) – he
describes the disciples in Mark as failures, because he is
attacking people who do not understand the cross or the resurrection? Or is the ending a literary device, whereby the
audience is addressed over the shoulders of the women, and
the question is left in the air, Was the young man right? Is

Christ risen? One could compare the way in which the book of Jonah ends with a question.

I do not intend to comment on these or on any other interpretations of the end of Mark, because it seems to me that it is important to separate, as far as we possibly can, two kinds of question: What is the text? and, Why was it written? There were terms that described the distinction, but they are seldom used now: lower criticism and higher criticism.[10] The end of Mark belongs more to the former than to the latter.

I suspect that the reason why there is still opposition to the view that 16.8 was the intended ending of the Gospel is because people do not want to buy any of the explanations that have been offered with it as a package deal. There is no need to attach the question of the ending to any particular explanation; it is a question on its own.

Nor, of course, is there any need to think that, if Mark meant to end there, it was because he did not believe in the resurrection. It would not follow that if he did not include resurrection appearances, he did not believe that Christ was risen. He refers to the resurrection directly or indirectly at the following points in his book: 8.31, 38; 9.9, 31; 10.34; 12.10–11, 18–27, 35–7; 13.26–7; 14.28, 58, 62; 16.6. Did he need to say more?

Notes

1   R. H. Lightfoot, *Locality and Doctrine in the Gospels* (London: Hodder & Stoughton, 1938); *The Gospel Message of St Mark* (Oxford: Clarendon Press, 1950).

2   See, for example, C. E. B. Cranfield, *The Gospel According to Saint Mark* (Cambridge: Cambridge University Press, 1959), pp. 470f.

3   F. L. Cross (ed.), *The Oxford Dictionary of the Christian Church*, 2nd edn (Oxford: Oxford University Press, 1974), s.v. 'Marcan Hypothesis'.

4   Bruce Metzger (ed.), *A Textual Commentary on the Greek New Testament*, corrected edn (London: United Bible Societies, 1975), p. 126, n. 7.

5 N. T. Wright, *Who was Jesus?* (London: SPCK, 1992), p. 85.

6 R. H. Gundry, *Mark: A Commentary on His Apology for the Cross* (Grand Rapids, MI: Wm B. Eerdmans, 1993).

7 There had, however, been an article in the *Journal of Theological Studies* 27 (July 1926), pp. 407ff., by R. R. Ottley on the use of *gar* as the last word in a sentence.

8 J. M. Creed, 'The Conclusion of the Gospel according to Saint Mark', *Journal of Theological Studies* 31 (1930), pp. 175ff.

9 I take it that by 'codex *a*' Creed meant to refer to the Old Latin codex Vercellensis; as far as I can see, no other writer includes *a* as a witness to the ending at 16.8, and Nestle-Aland, *Novum Testamentum Graece*, 26th edn, p. 712, says that it includes Mark 15.15—16.20.

10 See Cross, *Oxford Dictionary of the Christian Church*, s.v. 'Higher Criticism'.

8

Some Problems with Matthew

IN 1996, THE GENERAL SYNOD of the Church of England decided to adopt the Revised Common Lectionary (Common Worship Lectionary) for use on Sundays and principal feasts and festivals. One feature of this lectionary is 'The Liturgical Gospel'; there is a three-year cycle, and the Gospel readings at the Sunday eucharist each year are generally taken from one of the first three Gospels: thus in the year beginning on Advent Sunday AD 2000, the Gospel of Luke is used; in the following year, the Gospel of Matthew, and in the year beginning on Advent Sunday in 2002, the Gospel of Mark.

One might expect this method of allocating Gospels to years to have the result of drawing the preacher's and the congregation's attention to the differences between these three books; this would not follow inevitably, but it might happen in places where the preacher chose on occasion to refer to the individual characteristics of the evangelists: 'This is a point that Matthew stresses'; 'Mark frequently uses this word'; 'It is thanks to Luke that we know about this'; and so on.

If this is what happens, will congregations begin to have views about the Gospels, positive or negative? Can you imagine people saying, in the final weeks of the Sundays after Trinity: 'I am so much looking forward to Mark next year', or 'What a pity we are coming to the end of Luke'? And, should this be the case, how do we expect the three Gospels to be appreciated?

It is likely that Luke would be the most popular. It has the best-known parables, the annunciation to Mary, the

79

shepherds and the most quoted sayings from the cross. In some parishes, it was chosen as the Gospel to be distributed in 2000, presumably because it was thought to be the most accessible. There might be some who would prefer Mark to the other three; its public recitation, both in theatres and in churches, has held audiences' attention; the author was a skilled storyteller. But what about Matthew, the Liturgical Gospel for 2001–2, and every third year thereafter?

For centuries, it was Matthew that was the Gospel that was read most frequently at the Sunday eucharist in the West. In compiling the First Prayer Book of Edward VI in 1549, Cranmer apparently took over more or less wholesale an arrangement of readings that was already in use in the pre-Reformation Church, and the figures were:

Matthew	19	(36%)
Luke	16	(31%)
John	15	(29%)
Mark	2	(4%)

These proportions remained in the Book of Common Prayer of 1662, and the first change did not come until 1980, with the publication of the two-year cycle of readings in the Alternative Service Book. The figures then were:

John	42	(38%)
Luke	30	(27%)
Matthew	27	(24%)
Mark	12	(11%)

That is to say, Luke and Mark retained their positions in second and fourth place respectively, while John took over at the top of the table and Matthew fell to third. What explanation can we find for this decline in the popularity of what had previously been the most-used Gospel?

There is no problem about its previous popularity. It was one of the only two Gospels thought to have been written by one of the Twelve (the other being John); it was the only

Gospel to include the word 'church'; it was the easiest Gospel in which to find a particular passage one was searching for, because it was largely arranged by topic; it was the only Gospel that contained the instruction to baptize in the name of the Trinity; it included statements about the authority of the Twelve (and, particularly, of Peter); it provided a procedure for the excommunication of a member of the congregation.

Perhaps simply to list some of these Matthean features provides the answer to the question why Matthew's Gospel was less popular in 1980 than it had been throughout the previous Christian centuries. The way in which Matthew pictured Jesus had changed; Matthew's concerns were no longer our concerns, nor were they what we thought were those of Jesus.

It may have been the case that those who compiled the 1980 Sunday lectionary were influenced by a changed attitude to the relationship between Matthew and Mark. Apparently it was a new idea, which first appeared in the early nineteenth century, that Mark was the earlier Gospel, Matthew the later; and that Matthew had used almost all of Mark in the production of his longer work. He had done this without acknowledgement. Our ideas about declaration of sources are different from those of writers in the ancient world, and we can understand that and accept it, without criticism of any kind. It does, however, leave us with a problem: what Matthew did in his use of Mark in effect misled readers of these two Gospels for eighteen hundred years; and there have been people who have suffered at the hands of ecclesiastical authorities for maintaining Marcan priority.

Matthew, it is now thought, produced an enlarged edition of Mark, and one of the additional elements in the new edition is the formula with which Matthew introduces quotations from Scripture; for example: 'All this happened in order to fulfil what the Lord declared through the prophet . . .' (1.22). This formula, in slightly different words, occurs eleven times in Matthew. He read the Hebrew Scriptures as predictions of the events in the life and death of Jesus. The virginal

conception, the birth at Bethlehem, the death of the Inno-
cents, the flight into Egypt and the return to Nazareth, the
ministry of John the Baptist, the ministry of Jesus in the land
of Zebulun and Naphtali, and so on. Here again, we can
understand why it was that the first followers of Jesus related
their beliefs about him to Scripture. Jesus, they said, was the
Yes to all the promises of God, and these promises were to be
found in the Scriptures. We can compare their use of the
theme of fulfilment with that of the writers for the Dead Sea
Scrolls and their Teacher of Righteousness. What seems to us
problematic is the detailed application of this belief in
Matthew's book, and its use by Matthew to alter and extend
the Marcan narrative. When he is faced with a contradiction
between what Mark had written and what was said in Scripture, Matthew follows Scripture rather than Mark. Scripture
was God's word; Mark was a book that could be corrected;
that was what Matthew was doing. So it was two animals, not
one, that Jesus sent his disciples to fetch (Zechariah 9.9);
there were healings in the temple, of the blind and the lame,
unlike the time when David took Jerusalem (2 Samuel
5.6–8); it was gall, not myrrh, that was mixed with the wine
the soldiers offered to Jesus at Golgotha (Psalm 69.21 in the
Greek translation). We can blame ourselves for concentrating
too much on the question, Did it happen? But there is no
doubt that Matthew has added to the problems that lie in wait
for his present-day expositor. His Gospel requires more
explanation than either Mark's or Luke's.

As Matthew seems to have understood it, the authority of
Scripture involved more than prophecies of Christ; the law of
Moses was still binding upon the followers of Jesus. A com-
parison of Matthew with Mark shows that in passages where
Mark seems to follow Paul in his attitude to the law, Matthew
changes what was in his source. Mark had commented that
Jesus' saying about defilement meant that he declared all
foods clean; Matthew omits Mark's comment, and rearranges
the whole passage so that what Jesus said applied (only?) to
the custom of hand-washing (Matthew 15.1–20). In Mark,
Jesus had said that no commandment was greater than the

commandments to love God and neighbour; in Matthew, this is changed to: Everything in the law and the prophets hangs on those two commandments (22.34–40). The law must be taken as a whole; not a letter, not a dot, is to be ignored (5.18).

In the second century, Irenaeus knew about Christians who would accept only Matthew's Gospel; and these seem to have been Jewish Christians, who continued to keep the law. They apparently interpreted Matthew as meaning that the law of Moses was still to be observed. One of the problems of the early history of the canon of Christian Scripture is how Matthew's Gospel came to be accepted by churches that followed Paul rather than the church in Jerusalem; already in the first and second decades of the second century, Ignatius of Antioch seems to have been referring to Matthew as 'The Gospel'. The decline in Matthew's popularity in the modern world may be due in part to the realization that there is in it an element of re-judaization. This would explain the alteration of 'kingdom of God' to 'kingdom of heaven' in the vast majority of the instances where the term is used in this Gospel.

To us, Matthew is still the Jewish rabbi, and for all our intentions of goodwill toward Judaism, we cannot avoid the thought that he and his original congregations took some things far more seriously than we do. Must he not (we wonder) despise us and the laxity of our lives?

In what may seem to us a paradoxical manner, Matthew's continuing Judaism is one of the roots of his anti-Judaism. It has often been said that his Gospel is both the most Jewish and the most anti-Jewish of the four. The quarrels that are most bitter are between those who are closest to one another: the wounds we get in the house of our friends. In Matthew's experience, Jesus had not come to bring peace, but a sword: a man set against his father, a daughter against her mother, a daughter-in-law against her mother-in-law; his enemies were under his own roof. Like Paul, he had great grief and unceasing sorrow for his kinsfolk who had not followed him into faith in Christ. We may think, however, that he had this less under control than Paul.

He has organized his book according to his belief that the whole Jewish people, through their rejection of Jesus, were the cause of the destruction of Jerusalem by the Romans in AD 70. This event was God's answer to their acceptance of responsibility: His blood be on us and on our children (27.25).

Matthew summarizes the ministry of Jesus in three words: teaching, preaching and healing (chapters 4–9). Then the Twelve are sent to preach and to heal, but to Israel only (chapter 10). In the next section of the Gospel, Matthew has collected together passages that describe the rejection of the message by 'this generation' (chapters 11, 12); and it is followed by the parables of fruitful and unfruitful sowing, wheat and weeds, good and worthless fish (chapter 13). It is at this point that Matthew says that Jesus dismissed the crowds and went into the house where he expounded the parable to his disciples (13.36), and in a sense this is the turning-point of the story; from now on, Jesus will prepare his disciples to be the officers of his Church and he will send them, with authority to teach, to the gentiles, not to the Jews (28.19f.). Any mission to Jews is only to aggravate their guilt; they will be punished for all the innocent blood spilt on the ground, from the time of Abel to that of Zechariah son of Berachiah (23.35f.). The quest for the origin of the Church's attitude to the Jews throughout most of its history may well be found in Matthew's book.

He was a writer who saw everything in sharp contrast, a practical dualist, fond of parables that contained antithetical elements. The conclusion to the Sermon on the Mount sets before the reader the alternatives: the narrow gate or the wide gate, the constricted road or the broad road, destruction or life, false prophets or (by implication) true prophets, good trees with good fruit or poor trees with bad fruit, some people who only say Lord, Lord or others who also do the will of the Father, those who build on rock or those who build on sand, the house that survives rain, floods and winds or the house that falls.

A further result of his anti-Jewishness is his removal from

the narrative of any sense of ambiguity. He leaves no place for honest doubt or unbelief. Anyone who does not believe is simply ignoring facts, and such blindness is culpable. Herod knows that the King of the Jews has been born, and where he has been born; the star and the astrologers and the chief priests and scribes have told him; his response is the massacre of the boys in Bethlehem. The chief priests know that Jesus has been raised from the dead; the guards have reported to them, and there have been two earthquakes and the resurrection of the saints; their response is to bribe the soldiers to lie.

The present-day reader of Matthew feels compelled to say 'But surely it is never as simple as that. Does God really reveal himself in power? Isn't ambiguity an essential element in revelation? Where is the foolishness of God and the weakness of God? Hasn't Matthew condemned those who do not believe to damnation?' And certainly a case can be made for saying that there is more about hell in Matthew than in the whole of the rest of the New Testament. For example:

wailing and grinding of teeth	in Matthew	6 times	in the rest of the NT	once
Gehenna	in Matthew	7 times	in the rest of the NT	5 times
eternal punishment	in Matthew	once	in the rest of the NT	never

It may well be, therefore, that Matthew's Gospel will be the one we find it hardest to appreciate, and the years when it is the Liturgical Gospel the years that require most explanation. Perhaps we can explain it as the product of a particular and terrible situation, such as we hope that we ourselves may never experience. The author was adapting an earlier Gospel (Mark's) for congregations which, unlike Mark's, continued to keep the Mosaic law and obeyed the command to show themselves far better than the scribes and Pharisees; they hoped to be among the few who would enter life by the narrow gate. They had no friends, either among the churches that had been founded by Paul and followed his teaching with regard to the law, or among the Jews who did not believe, with them, that Jesus was the Christ.

Their situation is reflected in their theology, with its antithetical dualism and lack of hope for the majority of humanity – the many who are on the broad road to eternal damnation. All they have is membership of a new institution, founded by Jesus, which has officers to whom he has given authority, and that authority will be endorsed by God himself.

Biblical criticism, it has been said, is the preacher's best friend. What we need to see now is how this insight might apply in the case of Matthew's Gospel. All it seems to have done so far is to turn us away from that book, and perhaps explain why others have done so too.

But that is not at all how it is. Historical criticism, as applied to Scripture, shows us both what is not to be believed, and what is to be believed. There is nothing wrong in picking and choosing; that is in fact how we live. And it is how Paul thought his recipients in Thessalonica should live, when he wrote what is possibly the oldest surviving Christian document:

> Do not stifle inspiration
> or despise prophetic utterances,
> but test them all;
> keep hold of what is good
> and avoid all forms of evil.
> (1 Thessalonians 5.19–22)

Thus it is possible to distinguish between what is probably historical and what is almost certainly legendary, and not to treat the latter as if it were the former; and between the moral statements that seem to us to belong to a past way of life, and those that do not.

In the case of Matthew, the situation that produced some of his characteristic attitudes that we have been considering also led him to a position in which he could see other things more clearly than perhaps anyone else before him. Unpopularity from all directions and persecution too forced him to see that following Jesus meant having no status in the world. Matthew is against anything that provides one with a reason for thinking oneself superior to anybody else.

The genealogy with which his book begins contains an incestuous couple, a prostitute and an adulterer and an adulteress; as far as we know, no one had said before Matthew, that Rahab the harlot married Salmon and was thus the great-great-grandmother of King David. Jesus was conceived out of wedlock and Joseph was forbidden to do anything to conceal this. The Baptist had warned people not to use descent from Abraham as a reason for avoiding repentance: God can make children for Abraham out of stones; and though John wants to exempt Jesus from baptism, Jesus will not accept it: It is right for us to do all that God requires, which includes identifying himself with those who repent of their sins.

The beatitudes describe the followers of Jesus as those who have none of the advantages that are normally valued so highly; instead, the blessed are the poor and the downtrodden, those who mourn and those who are hungry and thirsty, those who do not take sides but make peace and are persecuted for it. What they will have is insults, persecution and slander. Religion itself will not provide them with status; that is why almsgiving, prayer and fasting must be performed in secret. They are in no position to judge others, because they have nothing on which to seat themselves in judgement. They cannot demand that people pay them what they owe, because they themselves are discharged bankrupts and they have remitted all debts owed to them. They must not be addressed with honorific titles such as 'rabbi' or 'father'. They must not suppose that gifts of preaching or exorcism or performing miracles will provide them with an entrée into the kingdom of heaven.

According to one interpretation of the final parable in the Gospel, the brothers and sisters of Jesus are described as people who are hungry and thirsty, away from home and naked, sick and in prison. They depend on others (outside their community) for their basic needs. This is their ultimate humiliation.

Matthew wrote out of the situation into which following Jesus had brought him and those for whom he was writing. He was a member of a sect that was hated and despised, and that would, in a fairly short time (perhaps a century, perhaps slightly longer) disappear from off the face of the earth. He knew all about the love of popularity that afflicts most people, and he knew that true religion could give you no relief from it; it only made it more difficult.

Providence had led him into a desperate situation, but he had accepted it and learned from it. Providence is not fastidious; it will use anything to achieve its end, which is to teach us the truth. Maybe, given the way we are, that is the only means by which it can do it.

A year with Matthew as the Liturgical Gospel may not be an easy year, either for the preacher or for the congregation. It may call for much explanation of the text. And if we can see the direction in which Matthew is pointing his readers, away from popularity and acceptance, towards the one Teacher, the Messiah, who drags his followers down to his own level, that too will not make for an easy year. But then Matthew never thought that it was his job to give us one.

9

The Blessed Virgin Mary

THE TASK OF THE PREACHER is to proclaim the gospel; and in this case, to proclaim the gospel as it is presented to us in the person of Mary, the mother of Jesus. The question that must be addressed is, How should we think about the Lord's mother, so as to hear, through her, the good news of God? What aspect of the gospel does she present? What is there about her that will lead us to faith in her Son?

Hearing the gospel is always a matter that lies outside our control. We cannot simply decide to believe. Hearing the good news is an act of God, symbolized in the Gospel stories of miraculous gifts of sight to the blind and hearing to the deaf. In the matter of the mother of Jesus we shall need God's grace to an exceptional degree. We enter a minefield and only a power outside us will preserve us from detonating our own destruction.

For, ever since the sixteenth century, Christians in the West have been deeply divided in their attitude to Mary: some have continued to address the Virgin in their prayers, and have clarified what is to be believed about her in infallible statements. Others have not asked for her prayers, nor held any clearly formulated beliefs about her. Anyone brought up in a place where Catholics and Protestants live side by side in great numbers knows that Mary is one of the most serious causes of division: one side says the other does not believe enough; they reply that their opponents believe too much.

We hope and we pray that in the third millennium all Christians will return to greater unity. But how can they do so in this respect? So it is a matter of urgency that we ask, What is the gospel that Mary proclaims? What aspects of the good news does she embody?

Three persons with proper names are mentioned in the creeds: Jesus, Pontius Pilate and Mary. We know more about Jesus than we do about Pilate; we know more about Pilate than we do about Mary. For Jesus, we have mainly Christian writings from the first century. For Pilate, we have the Jewish writers, Josephus and Philo. For Mary, we have – what?

The earliest reference to her in the surviving literature is a letter from Paul to the churches of Galatia, probably written in the mid-fifties. All he says is that God sent his Son, born of a woman, born under the law, in order that we might attain the status of sons of God. God's Son had human birth, in order that we might become children of God and address him as Father. All Paul means by 'born of a woman' is to emphasize the humanity of Jesus, not to say anything specific about the Lord's mother. God deals with us through one of us, because we are all, like Jesus, born of women.

The next Christian writer after Paul whose work has survived, as most people now think, is Mark, the author of the oldest Gospel. The mother of Jesus is referred to, in this book, on two, or possibly three, occasions. The family of Jesus, that is, his mother and his brothers, say that he is out of his mind, and set out to take charge of him; when they arrive at the house where he is teaching, they stand outside and send in a message asking him to come out to them. He says, Who are my mother and my brothers? Not those who are outside the house, but those who are inside, sitting in a circle about him: Here are my mother and my brothers. Whoever does the will of God is my brother and sister and mother. A strange story, typically Marcan: ironic, caustic and totally unsentimental. Mark always says what you least expect. Surely one should honour one's mother? The gospel, as Mark understands it, is like salt. He makes no concessions to our weakness, but rubs salt into our wounded humanity. Family relationships are over, now; the only hope is in a new family – those who follow the crucified man.

The second time that the mother of Jesus is mentioned in Mark is again for the purpose of telling us who Jesus is not. In the synagogue in his home town, people say, 'Is not this the carpenter, the son of Mary, the brother of James and Joses and Judas and Simon? Are not his sisters here with us?' Those who speak thus do not believe in him: Mark says so, explicitly. They define Jesus in terms of his physical relations, his mother and his brothers and his sisters. And all they can see in him is his occupation: the carpenter. What should be believed is that Jesus is the Son of God, as the voice from heaven has said; he is the one who has come to destroy the demons, as one of them has said. A point to note is that this passage, in the sixth chapter of Mark, is the earliest evidence for the name of the mother of the Lord: this is the first place where Mary is mentioned by name.

The third reference to her in Mark is disputed. There is a Mary mentioned three times at the end of the book, at the crucifixion, at the burial and at the tomb on the third day. She is referred to first as Mary the mother of James the younger and of Joses; then as Mary the mother of Joses; and finally as Mary the mother of James. She is one of the group who disobey the young man's instruction to tell his disciples; she is one of those who said nothing to anyone, because they were afraid. Mark may have mentioned these women, because, as he saw it, they fulfilled a prophecy in the Psalm,

> My friends and companions shun me in my sickness
> and my kinsfolk keep far off.
> (Psalm 38.11)

They stand far off from Jesus as he dies, alone, rejected by the leaders of Israel and deserted by his family and his disciples and by God himself. What Jesus does, he does for everybody; therefore he does it alone. In a theology of such rigorous negativity there was no place for a positive attitude to the Lord's mother.

All Mark has provided us with is the name of Mary, the names of his brothers; the existence of his sisters; and the gulf that there was between them and him: they thought he was out of his mind.

Mark had begun his Gospel with John the Baptist; he had not attempted to write a description of events before that – the birth of Jesus or his early years. Matthew and Luke, Mark's successors and editors, expanded his narrative in both directions, with resurrection appearances at the end, and with infancy narratives at the beginning. These birth stories are examples of a different kind of writing from most of the rest of the first three Gospels: angels appear, and play an essential part in the plot; people are told in advance who the baby will become and what he will do. There are miracles: of a star and a virginal conception. These are legends, and their purpose is literary: to inform the readers of the books from the start about the identity of the principal character. Matthew, as in the rest of his Gospel, stresses the fulfilment of Scripture; Luke shows how Jesus fulfils the promise of a final Son of David.

These infancy narratives tell us what to believe about Jesus; but do they give us historical information about the circumstances of his birth? Professor E. P. Sanders, in his 1993 book *The Historical Figure of Jesus*, points out that the Matthean and Lucan stories are incompatible; they cannot both be historical; he and many others think that neither is. Some scholars hold that there is an historical element behind the two accounts; others think that any agreement between them is the result of dependence – that is, Luke knew Matthew's book, and reworked Matthew's stories of annunciation, virginal conception and visitors to see the child, according to his own purpose and theology. A. N. Wilson, in his 1992 book, *Jesus*, was characteristically outspoken on this subject:

> It is hard to think of a body of stories which is less edifying. For sheer silliness, they are almost unrivalled. . . . If you read the infancy narratives in Matthew [and] Luke . . . and these narratives alone, and if you knew nothing of other Christian writings or teachings, it would not occur to you that the Christian religion had any claim to be morally serious. (p. 90)

Nor shall we find further historical information about the mother of Jesus in the Fourth Gospel, or in the Acts of the Apostles or in Revelation – the only other books of the New Testament in which she is mentioned. In John's Gospel, she appears at the wedding at Cana, and at the crucifixion. Her name, Mary, is not used; instead, she is referred to as 'the mother of Jesus', and her role seems to be symbolic: she stands for Israel as the witness to Christ; she sees the inadequacy of the old order (They have no wine); she commands obedience to her son (Do whatever he says); finally she is entrusted with the representative disciple (Behold, your son). And it is also as a symbol that she appears in Revelation: the woman robed with the sun, with the moon beneath her feet; the mother of the child who is destined to rule all nations; the mother also of those who keep God's commandments and maintain their witness to Jesus. In Acts, she is mentioned once in the first chapter in a list of members of the church in Jerusalem. That is all there is in the New Testament.

Anyone looking at this must be struck by the apparent disproportion between what can be known about the mother of Jesus from a historical point of view, and what is said about her in prayers, hymns and the doctrines of the Church; the place she occupies in Christian art; and the attention she has received in Christian architecture. How can so much have come out of so little? If we go to practically any art gallery in Europe, we shall see her looking at us from the picture frames, as she holds her child in her arms. If we go to almost any medieval cathedral, we shall be shown the Lady Chapel at the east end of the building. There are churches where, three times a day, the bell is rung for the Angelus, with its three Hail Marys. The Sunday Missal of the Catholic Church contains prayers to Our Lady: Angelus, Magnificat, Memorare, Salve Regina and others.

All that we know for certain – as certain as is possible in knowledge of the past – is that the man called Jesus, who was crucified under Pontius Pilate in Judaea in the thirties of the first century, was the son of a woman called Mary. This is the seed from which all the rest has grown. Hang on to this, because this may be the answer to our question, What is the gospel that Mary represents? How does she embody the good news of God?

It is Luke, of all the New Testament writers, who devotes most space to Mary. It is in his book, only, that we read the story of the annunciation to Mary: Gabriel coming to the house where she was, and saying to her, 'Hail most favoured one. The Lord is with you.' What does Luke tell us about Mary, before this? Only that she was betrothed to Joseph, a descendant of David; and that she lived in Nazareth.

Luke's silence about Mary is impressive. Usually, when he introduces a new character to his narrative, he tells us something about the person. Zechariah and Elizabeth, the parents of John the Baptist, were upright and devout. Simeon too was upright and devout, awaiting the restoration of Israel. Anna never left the temple, but worshipped there night and day. The centurion at Capernaum had built a synagogue for the Jews. The woman whose many sins were forgiven had loved much. Stephen was a man of faith and full of the Spirit. Cornelius was devout, a worshipper of God, and a man of great generosity. Barnabas and Saul were praying and fasting, before they were sent off on a mission. But Luke says nothing at all about either the character or the good works of Mary. Nor does he say what she was doing when the angel came to her. In Christian art she is often represented as praying, or reading a book. Luke does not say so. His one and only explanation is, God has shown her his favour. And about God's favour, nothing further can be said: it is in itself the answer to the question, Why?, that excludes all other answers. It is a way of saying, We do not know why, except that this is how it was. It does not refer to previous performance, to worthiness, to suitability, or to any antecedent condition. Grace is grace, and that closes the question.

In the history of the doctrines about Mary in the Church, much comes out of very little. And this is also how it all began, according to Luke: everything came out of nothing.

Luke gives us no description of Mary, no explanation of why she was chosen. Only: that God chose her. We cannot penetrate his mind, or give reasons for his choices. In the Magnificat, the speaker (whether it is Mary or Elizabeth does not matter) – the speaker says

> He who is mighty has done great things for me.

As we look at the position that Mary has held in the minds of Christians, both in the East and in the West, we cannot deny that great things have been done for her. Someone about whom nothing is known for certain – except that she had a son who was called Jesus – has become the best known and most loved of all the women who have ever lived.

Can we see also that it is precisely because we do not know about her, that we can relate to her? If she had had achievements and gifts, they would only have separated her from us. It is her absence of merit that makes her accessible. She has nothing we might envy, nothing to arouse our jealousy.

Allow me to indulge in one speculation. If we are ever to hear her speak to us, it will, I suppose, be in the language in which we were born: Parthians, Medes and Elamites . . . English people, Scots, Welsh and Irish too. If Luke is right, and Mary's home was Nazareth in Galilee – Nazareth, whence nothing good was expected to come – she would, presumably, like Peter, have spoken with a northern accent; her speech would have betrayed her origin. We shall hear her, therefore, speaking with the long 'o's of our own north country in book and look; short 'a's in grass and dance; and those resounding final 'g's in singing and ringing. She will be eminently accessible – still the lassie from among the sticks of Galilee.

We shall all have come a long way, by then. The Lord will have done great things for us also, whereof we shall rejoice. We shall all be God's *nouveaux riches*, his *parvenus*; upstarts, exalted by God. Bumped up mud. We shall not be aware so much of the difference between her and us, as of what we and she all have in common: that it is the favour of God that has exalted us all; this favour that is unaccountable and inexplicable.

The good news of God which Mary embodies, the gospel which she proclaims, is that God is mighty, and has done great things already. He made everything out of nothing, when he created the world. He made the mother of his Son out of a Galilean girl from Nazareth, when he redeemed it. He has taken us and sanctified us though we are dust – and it is all of his favour and his grace. The good news of Mary is the good news of God, mighty and bountiful.

10

Eating People

THIS CHAPTER IS ABOUT A PROBLEM that has been with me for many years. It all began when I asked a friend why he took his family to church on Sunday mornings, but never stayed for the service – though I knew that he sometimes went to evensong. He said, Because it is always parish communion. I asked him what was wrong with that, and he said, I am not a cannibal. He said that he knew enough about comparative religion and eating habits in various parts of the world to be quite sure that he could never make sense of a service that involved eating somebody's body and drinking his blood. However much it was spiritualized, or said to be symbolic, he could not, he said, make religious sense of this particular practice.

I cannot remember exactly what I said, but I think it was to the effect that Jews were not cannibals, and that Jesus and his disciples were all Jews.

That was how the problem began; I could have expressed it then in two ways:

First, as a matter of history, how did it come about that first-century Jews told a story about a Jew who invited, or commanded, other Jews to eat bread about which he said, This is my body; and to drink wine about which, in some traditions, he said, This is my blood? How could this have happened in a Jewish society?

Second, as a matter of pastoral practice, how should we explain to late twentieth-century intelligent liberal-minded Europeans like my friend, the meaning of what we are doing at the eucharist, when we eat what is said to be the body of

Christ and drink what is said to be his blood? How do we deal with the charge that we are being cannibals?

My hope at that time, when the problem started, was that if we could answer the historical question (What did they mean in the first century?) we should be well on the way to answering the second question (How can we explain what we are doing today?).

One of the assumptions on which all modern study of the New Testament is based, is that the original authors of the texts, and the characters about whom they were writing, were people of that time and place, and that they used the ideas and languages that were available to them. This, I take it, is what we mean by the *historical* study of the New Testament. So, if we want to know what words and sentences meant to people who used them in the first century, we shall need to have other examples of the use of the word, or similar sentences, from as close as we can get to that time and place. And it would always be possible to say, This could not have meant that, then, because this meaning was not available to people who lived then and there. One hesitates to give an example, because it is so easy to be mistaken about the facts; but would it not be true to say that nobody thought that the heart pumped blood round the body, until William Harvey said so, in 1628; therefore anyone who suggested that, in the New Testament, the heart meant a pump for distributing blood, must be wrong?

Another assumption, one that seemed to be uncalled for, was that the writers of the New Testament texts were a special case, because they were inspired; and that it was their inspiration that enabled them to think ideas that were not those of their contemporaries. We assume, I take it, that this is not how we should think of inspiration. It arranges what is to hand in new patterns; it does not normally involve thinking things that have never been thought of previously.

The study of Jesus in the last two hundred years seems to bear this out. (And of course it would, because we are in a (vicious?) circle: if we use historical methods, we shall inevitably confine ourselves to achieving historical results.) Certainly the languages and ideas of Jesus seem to have been those of first-century Galilean Jews: he talked about the kingdom of God, the age to come, eternal life, Beelzebul, Gehenna, the Son of Man; he used parables and riddles. There is nothing here that is original. What he meant by the expressions he used seems to have been what these expressions meant to his contemporaries. Originality is not a complete break with the past, but using traditional ideas in a new way.

If it is possible to shift the argument from words and sentences to manners and customs, then the only instance in the Gospels where the hypothesis that Jesus did not behave in a way that was out of the ordinary for a first-century Jew, is at the Last Supper. The text in Mark's Gospel is as follows:

> During supper he took bread, and having said the blessing he broke it and gave it to them, with the words: 'Take this; this is my body.' Then he took a cup, and having offered thanks to God he gave it to them; and they all drank from it. And he said to them, 'This is my blood, the blood of the covenant, shed for many.' (Mark 14.22–4, REB)

The problem is that eating human bodies was not a practice that was countenanced in Judaism. The story in 2 Kings 6 of the woman who cooked and ate her son during the siege of Samaria partly depends on the knowledge that cannibalism was horrific to Jews; so how could Jesus have given his disciples bread to eat, and said to them, This is my body? Drinking blood of any kind had been forbidden from the time of Noah, it was thought (Genesis 9.4ff.); so how could Jesus give them a cup of wine to drink, and when they had drunk it tell them that they had drunk his blood? The taboo against eating a human body and drinking any sort of blood was so strong, that it was impossible to imagine any Jew of the first, or any other, century seriously inviting his friends to do it – no more than I would pass you a glass of water and, after you had drunk it, say, This is my saliva.

There is a further problem, which is best put in the form of a question: Would it not be true to say that Judaism, unlike some other religions, did not make use of the idea of receiving grace through eating special foods, or drinking special drinks? If that were the case, then the idea of sacramental eating and drinking would have been unprecedented to first-century Jews; there would have been nothing like it in their tradition. The Passover lamb, and the cups of wine that were drunk at Passover, were not thought (as I understand it) to convey grace to the participants in a sacramental way.

The Jewish objection to drinking blood, and the relevance of this objection to the institution of the eucharist, have been known for a long time – eighty years, at least. Here, for example, is C. G. Montefiore in his commentary, *The Synoptic Gospels* (1909):

> I would also venture to suggest how difficult it is for us to believe that a Palestinian or Galilean Jew could have suggested that in drinking wine his disciples were, even symbolically, drinking blood. For the horror with which the drinking of blood was regarded by Jews is well known. (p. 236)

Montefiore goes on to quote Loisy's commentary on the synoptic Gospels (1907) and concludes that the original words of Jesus at the supper were simply, 'I shall not eat or drink again'; and he suggests that the eucharist was developed from this original saying of Jesus, by 'the inventive genius of Paul' (p. 332).

The same explanation of the origin of the eucharist came in a more recent book: Hyam Maccoby's *The Mythmaker* (1986). Maccoby, like Montefiore, thinks that Jesus, as a Jew, could not have spoken about eating his body and drinking his blood, but that this must have been invented by someone else, who was not a Jew by birth.

Maccoby believes that Paul was born a Gentile, and was converted to Judaism; that he never really understood Judaism or adopted its ideas fully; later, he became a Christian, and then his Hellenistic origins influenced the way in which he thought and wrote about Jesus. He sums up his chapter on 'Paul and the Eucharist' thus:

> A survey of the evidence thus confirms that Paul and no one else was the creator of the Eucharist. He gave authority to this new institution, which he actually derived from mystery religion, by adducing a vision in which he had seen Jesus at the Last Supper, giving instructions to his disciples about performing the Eucharistic rite. This vision of Paul's was later incorporated as historical fact into the Gospels, in the accounts given there of the Last Supper, and thus has been accepted as historical fact by the vast majority of New Testament scholars. The followers of Jesus in Jerusalem, who were pious Jews and would have regarded the idea of eating Jesus' body and drinking Jesus' blood as repugnant, never practised this rite, but simply took communal meals prefaced by the breaking of bread, in the manner sanctioned by Jewish tradition for fellowships within the general community of Judaism.
> (p. 118)

Both Montefiore and Maccoby find the idea that a Jew would have commanded people to eat his body and drink his blood historically impossible; and both adopt the hypothesis that the synoptic tradition of the institution of the eucharist derived from Paul, not from Jesus. While we might think that Mark was influenced by Paul, it would be difficult to see how Matthew's very Jewish congregation would have been persuaded, by Mark, or Paul, or by anyone else, to do something that was, apparently, so offensive to Jews. Matthew had gone through Mark altering almost every instance of 'the kingdom of God', to 'the kingdom of heaven', because, we are always told, of Jewish sensitivity; would he not have omitted the supper-words, if he had found them horrific? He did not; he copied Mark, adding to the form of the words over the bread and the cup.

The problem was, how could we explain a narrative that told us that Jesus had put people in the position of being commanded to do something that was abhorrent to them, in that it contravened a taboo that was based on a law which they believed God had given for all human beings, after the flood? The more writers like G. Vermes (whose book *Jesus the Jew* was first published in 1973) and E. P. Sanders in the 1980s, told us that Jesus was an observant Jew, who did not break the Mosaic law, the more difficult it became to think how he could have referred to eating his body, and drinking his blood. Yet there, in the synoptic Gospels and in 1 Corinthians 11, were the narratives. Paul did not have 'This is my blood', neither did Luke (in either the shorter or the longer text); whatever we thought about the original form of the cup-words, the words over the bread, in all four texts, were enough to create a problem: How could Jesus have invited people to eat him?

None of the commentaries on the synoptic Gospels, or on 1 Corinthians, that I came across ever seemed to address this problem; they never explained how a Jew could have said to other Jews that there was an analogy between eating bread and eating a human body, or between drinking wine and drinking human blood; and that his disciples must do both.

Round about this time, in the 1970s, the situation was made worse by the optional changes that the Church of England introduced into its authorized services. We had previously said, in a post-communion prayer:

> We most heartily thank thee, for that thou dost vouchsafe to feed us, who have duly received these holy mysteries, with the spiritual food of the most precious Body and Blood of thy Son our Saviour Jesus Christ . . .

What was proposed instead, and later authorized, was this:

> We thank thee for feeding us with the body and blood of thy Son Jesus Christ our Lord.

Both prayers say the same thing; but the older version (from the Book of Common Prayer of 1662) put a lot of words between 'feed us' and 'Body and Blood'; these words said that what we were fed with was 'the spiritual food of the most precious Body and Blood'. The new service simplified and abbreviated the prayer: we were to say that we had been fed 'with the body and blood'. Again, at the administration of communion, instead of a much longer form of words, one option was to say, 'The body of Christ', to which the communicant would reply 'Amen'; and 'The blood of Christ', to which the response was also 'Amen'.

The effect of these changes, it seemed to me, was to make the cannibalistic interpretation of the eucharist more likely. By 'cannibalistic' I understood the belief that through eating another human being, a friend or relation, or an enemy, you would acquire his soul-stuff: his virtues, powers, strength and courage. (See, for example, G. Hogg, *Cannibalism and Human Sacrifice*, 1958.) The doctrine of the eucharist that seemed to be being promoted by these changes in the liturgy was: The Life of Christ is made available to us now, through eating his body and drinking his blood. The act of communion is an act of feeding on Christ, body and blood, in order to receive his power.

The more it was said that the eucharistic gifts were really and truly Christ's body and blood, the worse it was, because the closer it came to cannibalism, in purpose and conception. But even if it were said that the gifts were symbols of Christ's body and blood, it was still difficult to see why they should be eaten and drunk. If Christ in flesh and blood were to walk into a room in which we were present, I used to think, some might kneel, or prostrate themselves; some might hug him or kiss him; but I could not imagine that anyone would bite him, or suck his blood, as the Kwakiutl Indians of North America were said to do to one another (Hogg, *Cannibalism*, chapter 3). Why should we do sacramentally what we would never think of doing literally? The need to have a bath gave meaning to baptism; the need to have authority conferred gave meaning to ordination; but I could see no need to eat somebody that would give meaning to the eucharist.

Help came from a totally unexpected quarter, when I was looking for something entirely different. It was a passage from R. E. Brown's commentary on John (Anchor Bible, 1966). He was arguing that the discourse on the bread of life in John 6 must have been displaced; it must, he said, have belonged originally to John's account of the supper. And the reason he gave was this: outside the context of the Last Supper, talk about eating people would have meant only one thing to Jews: to eat people was to be their enemy.

When I read that, I felt like Augustine in *The Confessions*:

> No further would I read; nor needed I: for instantly at the end
> of this sentence, by a light as it were of serenity infused in my
> heart, all the darkness of doubt vanished away. (viii. 28)

The problem, I thought, was solved. The language of eating, when it was eating people, was metaphorical, and the metaphor expressed hostility. Here is the passage from Brown:

> 'To eat someone's flesh' appears in the Bible as a metaphor for
> hostile action . . . In fact, in the Aramaic tradition transmitted
> through Syriac, the 'eater of flesh' is the title of the devil, the
> slanderer and adversary par excellence. The drinking of blood
> was looked on as an horrendous thing forbidden by God's law
> . . . Its transferred, symbolic meaning was that of brutal slaugh-
> ter . . . In Ezekiel's vision of apocalyptic carnage (xxxix 17), he
> invites the scavenging birds to come to the feast: 'You shall eat
> flesh and drink blood.' Thus, if Jesus' words in [John] vi 53 are
> to have a favorable meaning, they must refer to the Eucharist.
> (pp. 284f.)

Brown's argument was: Eating people by itself, without any interpretative context such as the institution of the eucharist, refers only to hostile action. Therefore the requirement that his disciples eat his flesh and drink his blood must have been said by Jesus in connection with the eucharist; had it not been, the words would have meant: You must be my destroy-ers; you must be the cause of my death.

But what I wondered was: Could not Jesus have used the metaphor of eating his flesh (or body), and drinking his blood, precisely in this hostile, destructive, adversarial sense, at the Last Supper? Could it not be that the original meaning of the eucharist was to be found in hostility, not in feeding on; in destruction, not in nutrition? Was not the way out of the highly unlikely cannibalistic sense to be found by taking the words over the bread and the wine metaphorically; meaning, You must be my adversaries?

In order to give any plausibility to such a suggestion, we should need to demonstrate two propositions: (i) that eating people in the adversarial sense was fairly common in the Old Testament; (ii) that the metaphor was still in use at the time when the New Testament was being written.

With regard to the Old Testament, anyone who is even moderately familiar with the Psalms will know that people are forever being eaten by their enemies and foes; they are consumed and swallowed up by those who hate them. There are at least twenty-eight instances of the vocabulary of ingestion in the Psalter where the thing being eaten is human; here are some obvious examples.

Evildoers . . . devour my people as if eating bread. (14.4)
Lions ravening and roaring open their mouths wide against
    me. (22.13)
Save me from the lion's mouth. (22.21)
Evildoers close in on me to devour me. (27.2)
We have swallowed him up. (35.25)
Zeal for your house has consumed me. (69.9)
Let no abyss swallow me up. (69.15)
They have devoured Jacob. (79.7)
The earth opened and swallowed Dathan. (106.17)
They would have swallowed us alive. (124.3)

I am told that the majority of the other instances of the language of eating people in the Old Testament are mainly in the prophets. Here is an example from Jeremiah:

> Israel, I am bringing against you a distant nation . . .
> They are all mighty warriors,
> their jaws are a grave, wide open,
> to devour your harvest and your food
> to devour your sons and your daughters,
> to devour your flocks and your herds,
> to devour your vines and your fig trees. (5.15–17)

One can see how, in the Old Testament, eating people expresses hostility, by noting the subjects of the eating verbs: Enemies and foes do it; the abyss does it; evildoers do it; lions, fire and the sword do it. You have to be against people, to eat them; eating people, in the Old Testament, is never a friendly or amiable activity. Moreover, there is no sense that the eater of people is nourished by it; all the emphasis is on the destruction of the victim, none on the benefit that accrues to the consumer. If we were to take the Old Testament for our guide to understanding the words of Jesus, we should have to say that when he made the disciples eat bread and said it was his body, he meant that he was making them responsible for his death.

There is no similar background to the New Testament for drinking blood, other than Ezekiel's birds, to which Raymond Brown referred; but there is one passage in the Old Testament that uses the expression in a way that is exactly parallel to what we may be finding for eating people; it is the story of David and the three mighty men in 2 Samuel 23.13–17 (and I am indebted to my friend Dr E. Whitaker for pointing it out to me). David had said: If only I could have a drink of water from the well by the gate at Bethlehem; and the heroic three made their way through the Philistine lines and brought the water to David. He refused to drink it, and poured it out to the Lord, saying: Can I drink the blood of these men who went at the risk of their lives? To drink this water would have been to take on responsibility for the men's lives. David attempts to dissociate himself from what they had done, by refusing to drink the water. Jesus, on the other hand, makes his disciples drink wine and tells them that they are responsible for his death: they have drunk his blood, he says, after they have done it. To drink someone's blood is to declare oneself the cause of that person's death.

If there are indeed enough instances of the metaphorical use of ingestion-words in the Psalms and the Prophets to provide a background for their use in the New Testament, is there any evidence that they were used in this way by New Testament writers, apart from the case in question, the words of Jesus at the Last Supper and in John 6? Is there enough evidence for us to say that it was a well-known and much used manner of speech in certain circles in the first century? Here is the evidence: Psalms that used this metaphor are quoted in the New Testament; for example 'Save me from the lion's mouth' (Psalm 22.21 in 2 Timothy 4.17); 'Your enemy the devil, like a roaring lion, prowls around looking for someone to devour' (Psalm 22.13 in 1 Peter 5.8); 'Zeal for your house will consume me' (Psalm 69.9 in John 2.17). There is also the dragon in Revelation 12.4 who wants to devour the woman's child. Paul can say to the Corinthians, and can assume that they will understand what he means, 'You put up with it if someone tyrannizes over you, if someone devours you' (2 Corinthians 11.20); and he can warn the Galatians, using a clutch of ingestion-words, 'If you bite and devour one another, take care that you are not consumed by one another' (Galatians 5.15). In the Letter of James, the rich are warned that when the end comes their flesh will be eaten by the corrosion of their silver and gold (James 5.3). There is also a passage in Mark where Jesus says that the scribes devour widows' houses (12.40) but this may not count; we are concerned with eating people, not eating houses.

The direction in which some of this evidence may be pointing is that eating people in a metaphorical sense, meaning to be their enemy, is primarily a Hebrew idiom, and that it appears in Greek only when there is a Hebrew background of some sort: either a quotation, or a Greek speaker thinking in Hebrew or Aramaic. In this way we might account for its occurrence in Paul and James and Revelation; and also in the four Gospels, both the synoptic accounts of the Last Supper and John 6. If we can go behind these accounts in the Gospels to the meaning of Jesus, it will have been that he commanded the disciples to take the bread and he passed them the cup to drink, in order to symbolize their responsibility for his death. To readers of Mark, this would be no surprise; they had heard Jesus say that he would give his life as a ransom for many (10.45); now, at the supper, they are made to act out his destruction for their salvation by means of eating and drinking. By this, they show themselves to be the brethren for whom Christ died.

Such an interpretation of the eucharistic words of Jesus might explain various passages in the New Testament, which we could note briefly:

1. Paul says to the Corinthians:

> When we bless the cup of blessing, is it not *koinōnia* of the blood of Christ?
> When we break the bread, is it not *koinōnia* of the body of Christ? (1 Corinthians 10.16)

What does *koinōnia* mean in this context? There is a passage in Matthew where Jesus says that those who build the tombs of the prophets say that if they had lived in the days of their fathers, they would not have been *koinōnoi* in the blood of the prophets – partners in crime; sharers in the murder of the prophets (23.30). So, in Paul, the cup of blessing is the means of sharing in responsibility for the death of Christ, and the breaking of the bread is the means of sharing in liability for his destruction. While we were enemies, we were reconciled to God by the death of his Son. The eucharist is the symbol both of enmity and of reconciliation: we destroy, and by doing so we are saved.

In 1 Corinthians 11 Paul says that anyone who eats the bread or drinks the cup of the Lord unworthily will be guilty of offending against the body and blood of the Lord; and that some have done this, and that is why many of them are feeble and sick, and a number have died. Not because there is any magic in the bread and the cup, but because the action itself symbolizes the guilt of murder; so to do it without faith in the saving power of this particular death is simply to proclaim oneself responsible for it, and to bear the consequences.

2. In Mark, the account of the supper is placed between two passages in which Jesus foretells the failure of disciples; before, he says: One of you will betray me; after the supper: You will all be scattered; and Peter will disown him three times. In between these predictions he makes them eat and drink, symbolizing both their failure and his destruction for them. This will become clear to the reader of Mark, as soon as they reach Gethsemane and they sleep while he prays. At the supper, however, they enact the meaning of the atonement in their mouths. Mark need not tell us more about the disciples after this; they have been made to perform the saving action; for Judas, as for the unworthy communicants at Corinth, it would have been better if he had not been born; the others will see the Son of Man when he comes in glory.

3. Matthew makes three alterations to Mark's text: he adds the command, Eat; he changes Mark's, They all drank of it, to: Drink from it, all of you; and he adds the interpretation, For the forgiveness of sins. His Jewish-Christian congregation apparently needed this expansion of the pre-Matthean wording: Jesus had commanded them to eat and to drink, however surprising they found it; and he had explained why they must do so: he saved his people from their sins by dying for them; they must acknowledge this by obeying the command and performing the metaphor.

4. The shorter text of Luke's account of the supper omits all reference to drinking blood. When he comes to write Acts, Luke will say that Christians are to abstain from blood (15.20, 29; 21.25); had the language of drinking blood lost its earlier meaning, when Luke wrote, and for the people for whom he wrote; and does that account for the origin of the shorter text?

5. John removes almost all traces of the institution of the

eucharist from his account of the supper, but introduces the foot-washing instead. Peter's unwillingness to allow Jesus to wash his feet represents the unwillingness of those who refuse to believe that Christ died for them. To reject the foot-washing is the same as to reject the eating of his flesh and the drinking of his blood (6.52–8). Is there, however, one trace of the eucharist still in John's account of the supper? – Jesus gives Judas something to eat, and Satan enters into him; he then goes out to set the events of the arrest and crucifixion in motion, obeying the command of Jesus: Do quickly what you have to do.

6. As the Church lost touch with its Jewish origins, it had to find new interpretations of the eating and the drinking which it continued to practise; an example of this is the pharmaceutical analogy in Ignatius of Antioch:

> . . . Breaking one bread, which is the medicine (*pharmakon*) of immortality and the antidote (*antidotos*) that we should not die but live for ever in Jesus Christ. (*Ephesians* 20.2)

From now on, attention will be focused more and more on what it is that is eaten and drunk, and less on why it should be done; the action ceases to be metaphorical and becomes literal.

7. The alternative to finding fresh interpretations of the eucharist was to abandon it altogether. Some writers think that this was the reason why the fourth evangelist did not include the institution in his account of the supper. Anyone reading John 6 and 13 who did not already know that Christians practised a rite that included eating bread and drinking wine, would not find it in the text, because it is not there.

But whether that view of the Fourth Gospel is accepted or not, there is another New Testament author who can be read as having a totally negative attitude to the eucharist; it is the writer of the Letter to the Hebrews, and the relevant passage is in the last chapter.

He warns his readers against strange teaching; the way in which we receive strength is through grace, not through food.

We have an altar, but we do not eat our sacrifice, because it is a sin-offering and sin-offerings are not eaten. The body of a sin-offering is burned outside the camp, where Jesus was crucified. The blood of sin-offerings is offered in the sanctuary, and Jesus is in heaven to do that. The sacrifices of the new covenant are not things to be eaten and drunk; they are praise of God and kindness and sharing one's possessions.

The question has sometimes been asked, Why did the author of Hebrews not mention the eucharist, when it seems so close to his theme? He did not mention it, because he did not believe in it; in fact, he wrote his Letter to show that there could be no sacramental eating and drinking because the sacrifice of Christ was a sin-offering; his death was the final Day of Atonement, a day for fasting.

In the 1970s, when my well-read friend explained that he could not attend parish communion because he was not a cannibal, I thought that the problem of eating people could be stated in two questions: What did Jesus mean? and, How can we explain it today?

1. Was Jesus using a metaphor when he spoke of eating his body and drinking his blood? Would that explain how a Jew could tell other Jews to do this? And did the metaphor express hostility and opposition?
2. If that were so, could we explain this in a way that would make it possible for people to take part in the eucharist today? I recall one person to whom I attempted to expound this idea and who said, If I thought that was what we did at holy communion, I would certainly never go again.

Additional note, 2001

I have included here the original paper that I read in 1991, more or less as it was then, and as it was printed in *Theology*. Hardly anyone agreed with the suggestion that it contained, though one or two people have said that they were glad that the subject had been raised.

Re-reading it now, ten years later, I wonder whether it might not have been better to have argued for a more limited thesis: that eating and drinking in Mark 14 were understood by Mark in the sense of taking responsibility for Christ's death. Mark's book is a text that we have, or at least have some confidence that we can reconstruct; the historical situation of the supper is far more of a problem.

I was surprised that some people found the idea in the paper so unusual, though I see now that I found it so myself when I wrote it. But what I think I had in mind was a hymn in *The English Hymnal* (1906, no. 7), also in *The New English Hymnal* (1986, no. 62), by Robert Bridges, originally published in *The Yattendon Hymnal* (1895–9). The hymn begins:

> Ah, holy Jesu, how hast thou offended . . . ?

The implied singer is thought of as looking at a representation of the crucifixion or imagining it, much as it is described in Mark 15:

> By foes derided, by thine own rejected,

that is, not only by the religious and the Roman authorities, but also by his own followers.

The first verse asks the question, and the second has the answer:

> Alas, my treason, Jesu, hath undone thee.
> 'Twas I, Lord Jesu, I it was denied thee:
> I crucified thee.

The singer of the hymn thereby identifies himself with Judas, one of the Twelve, and with Peter, the first of the Twelve. He and the followers of Jesus have united with the authorities, and he accepts responsibility for what happened.

The next verse recalls the Marcan language of shepherd and sheep, the Son who gave his life for the many, and the divine will and purpose that are behind it all:

> For man's atonement, while he nothing heedeth,
> God intercedeth.

Bridges' hymn is a translation and abbreviation of a much longer hymn by Johann Heermann (1585–1647), which begins:

Herzliebster Jesu, was hast du verbrochen

Catherine Winkworth had produced an English translation of it in 1863; it is based on a Latin original of the eleventh century, possibly by Jean de Fécamp (d. 1078), which begins:

Quid commististi, dulce puer, ut sic judicareris?

Is it possible that Mark wrote his Gospel so that those who heard it read could identify themselves with the various characters in the story who were, in one way or in another, responsible for the death of Jesus? We know that Paul read Genesis 3 as his own biography (Romans 7.7–12), and that he could say of Jesus, whom he had presumably never met, he 'loved me and gave himself up for me' (Galatians 2.20). The observance of the Passover involved the participants in reliving the events of the Exodus. Similarly, by eating and drinking, Mark's hearers share responsibility for the crucifixion, by performing actions that are associated with destruction.

For the full German text of *Herzliebster Jesu, was hast du verbrochen*, kindly made available for reproduction by Project Wittenberg, Project Coordinator the Reverend Bob Smith, see www.ctsfw.edu/etext/heerman

11

Christor the King

Christ the King

THE FEAST OF CHRIST THE KING is not a problem for
republicans. You can be as anti-monarchist as you want
and still keep this feast. Because what we celebrate on the
Feast of Christ the King is the crucifixion of Jesus.

There is so much to think about on Good Friday each year
that we have to have another day to deal with some of it. It is
too much for one occasion; so we have Christ the King at the
end of the liturgical year, to go back to the crucifixion and
remember what was said and done then. Christ reveals
himself as king, when he dies; his death is the way he reveals
his peculiar glory.

That is why republicans need have no problem with the
kingship of Christ. All that is objectionable about monarchy is
abolished in the crucifixion. A crucified man is not rich,
powerful, elitist, hereditary, exclusive, out of date, anomalous,
a hangover from the past, a cause of divisions in society, a
reason and a ground for snobbery. A crucified man is a non-
entity; all you can do with him is bury him. He has nothing,
not even any clothes. He cannot call anything his own. That is
what makes him king.

All our ideas about honour, power and majesty must be
controlled by the saying: *Many that are first shall be last, and the
last first.* The '*shall be*' there means, This is how God sees it;
this is how we must see it, too. God does not fit in with our
ways, or endorse our desires. We shall not be far wrong if we
adopt this rule: God's ideas are the exact opposite of ours;
therefore what we think good, he must think bad, and
whatever we think bad he must think good.

The way we are is: we would like to come out on top, be top people, do well, make a name for ourselves, be a success. That is what we think, and that is the opposite to what God thinks. By becoming first, you are in fact the last, the most misguided and pathetic person in the world. Poor you; you have succeeded. You have got what you wanted. You have received your reward. Nothing could be worse than that. There's nothing more dangerous than success, or more corrupting than power.

What we must long for is to be last. And it's not all that difficult, either. It's largely delusion that makes us think well of ourselves. We want to think we are better than others, so we do so; we see ourselves as we would like to be. But in fact we are not as good as all that. Courage! Doubt your good opinion of yourself. Rejoice in your inferiority. Be glad that you are a mess, a disaster. That is how it is meant to be. The last are the ones that are first.

People nowadays think that Mark's Gospel was written before the other three, and some people think that Mark's Gospel is the one that gets to the truth of Christianity by the quickest route. It is certainly a fact that Mark keeps the title king for Jesus until he gets to Good Friday, and then he has it six times, all from people who are mocking Jesus. They mock him for what he is, on the occasion when he is most clearly seen to be what he is: the last, a crucified man, a nobody, without any clothes, a corpse.

He has no power, no authority, no followers, no good opinion of himself, no sense that God approves of him. His mother and his brothers have said that he is mad; the Pharisees and Herodians wanted to destroy him because they thought he was bad; the scribes from Jerusalem thought he was in league with the devil; his disciples ran away; one betrayed him; the Rock disowned him, to a female slave. The Jewish Council said he was a blasphemer. He says, himself, God has abandoned him: God has not given him anything to say except that God has not given him anything to say; he will only quote Psalm 22. He cannot refute what people think. They think he is the last – the dregs, the bottom, the worst person who has ever lived, a deluded mad prophet, a would-be destroyer and rebuilder of the temple, a deranged healer, a neurotic, a psychopath. He's nobody. That's why he is the king: *the last shall be first.* You can hardly be more last than he was; you'll not be more first, either.

What a joy, then, to keep the feast of Christ the King! We do not feel any envy or jealousy. We do not think: I wish it were me – me the Messiah, not him. We think like that about everybody else's success: winning the National Lottery at the first go; winning the Booker Prize; getting an honorary degree; included in the Honours List. But none of us envies Jesus, or is jealous of his crucifixion. That is why he is king for all of us, and we can all be his happy subjects. He wins our loyalty by giving up his life for us, a ransom for everybody.

Why did he have to die? Why did his followers say, almost immediately after Good Friday, certainly within a year or two, *He died for us?* It was because he had not hung on to life, or goodwill, or self-respect, or the allegiance of his disciples, or thinking he was right, or anything that gave him a purchase over other people. He went so far down that it was impossible to imagine anyone going further. He got right down to the point where you could not go any lower. He kept nothing that could come between him and us. He let everything go, so that there would be no barrier to separate us from him.

And God said to him, That's right. You've got nothing now – nothing to call your own. You are the last and the least. So you can be king. Tell his disciples and Peter, They'll see you sitting at my right hand.

Notice the future tense: *They will see the Son of Man sitting at the right hand of the Almighty and coming with the clouds of heaven*, at the end of the world. But until then, we know him only as the crucified man, the one who was rejected by everybody, Godforsaken, the failure, the disaster.

Mark never lets Jesus come back on to the page of his book, after the crucifixion. He never wrote an account of resurrection appearances. The last words of Jesus, in Mark's book, are *My God, my God, why have you abandoned me?* This is the Jesus with whom we have to deal, all through the week, Monday to

Saturday. Because he has nothing, we need not be afraid of him. What frightens us in other people is their success, power, accomplishments, achievements. There is none of that, in Jesus crucified, only complete failure to persuade anybody, or make them see the point of what he said, or follow him.

This is why he is the king that no republican need refuse; he has none of the qualities that monarchs have had in history and none of their status. He is the total failure, the person no one can fear. God has made him our king.

Index of Names